Get to Know
ITALY

Michael Hill

Head of Social Studies Department,
St George's English School, Rome

HEB

HEINEMANN EDUCATIONAL BOOKS

OR 5.1.93

Heinemann Educational Books Ltd
Halley Court, Jordan Hill, Oxford Ox2 8EJ
OXFORD LONDON EDINBURGH
MADRID ATHENS BOLOGNA
MELBOURNE SYDNEY AUCKLAND
IBADAN NAIROBI GABORONE HARARE
KINGSTON PORTSMOUTH (NH) SINGAPORE

British Library CIP Data

Hill, Michael
    Get to know Italy.
    1. Italy
    I. Title
    945.092'8   DG417

    ISBN 0-435-39660-9

In the same series

Get to Know France
Get to Know Germany
Get to Know Spain

Photoset and printed in Malta by
Interprint Limited

Contents

Section one: The geography of Italy

1   Introduction to Italy

Italy in Europe

Italy is positioned right in the centre of the Mediterranean Sea. Its boot-shaped peninsula is separated from the rest of Europe in the north by the Alps. On the other three sides the country is surrounded by water, with the Adriatic Sea to the east, the Tyrrhenian Sea to the west and the Ionian Sea to the south. The two largest islands in the Mediterranean, Sicily and Sardinia, belong to Italy.

Mountains and plains

Italy is a very mountainous country and only a quarter of its territory is lowland. The Alps form an arc across northern Italy where the country's highest mountain, Monte Rosa (4633m), is located. This is one of many great peaks which are covered with snow all year round. In the area known as the Dolomites, the Italian Alps have some of the most rugged and spectacular scenery in Europe.

The Apennines form the 'backbone' of Italy and run the full length of the country. Although not as high as the Alps, they reach almost 3000 metres in the Gran Sasso.

Between the Alps and the Apennines is the *Pianura Padana*, or Northern Plain, Italy's largest piece of flat land. Stretching some 400 kilometres from east to west, it is made of sea deposits and materials washed down from the mountains by the River Po. There are smaller plains at various points along the Italian coastline—the Plain of Catania and the area around the Bay of Naples are two of the most important.

Volcanoes and earthquakes

The mountains of Italy are geologically young and unsettled. During the 20th century there have been several devastating earthquakes, including those of Messina in 1908, Friuli in 1976 and Basilicata and Campania in 1980. In these disasters thousands of people lost their lives and whole towns were destroyed.

Europe only has four active volcanoes and they are all in Italy. Mount Etna is the highest and covers a large area of eastern Sicily. Stromboli and Vulcano are small volcanic islands while Vesuvius, the best known of Italian volcanoes, dominates the skyline of the Bay of Naples. In other parts of the country there are crater lakes, hot springs and bubbling mud-pools which are the remains of volcanoes that have blown themselves into extinction.

Rivers

The Po is Italy's greatest river and is wide enough to be a major shipping route. It flows into the Adriatic Sea 650 kilometres from its source in the Alps, and has built up a marshy delta. In peninsular Italy the rivers which flow westwards into the Tyrrhenian are longer than

Questions

Look at the general map and answer the following:
1 Italy is a boot-shaped peninsula. Name two other Mediterranean countries which are on peninsulas.
2 How far is the south-eastern tip of Italy from Greece?
3 Why do you think that Sicily was easily overrun by the Arabs many centuries ago?
4 Why is Sardinia the most isolated part of Italy?

4

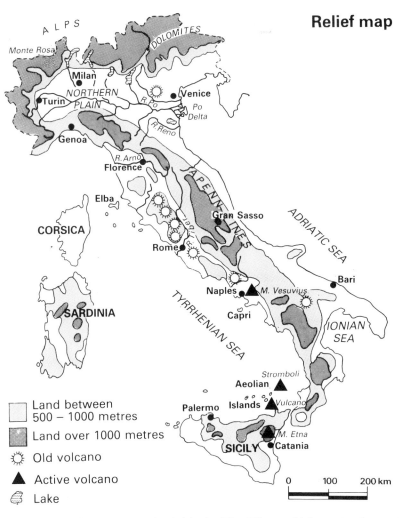

Relief map

Look at the relief map of Italy and answer the following:

1 How long is Italy from north to south?
2 How wide is the peninsula at its narrowest part?
3 Which large island is close to Italy but not a part of it?
4 In which part of Italy are the volcanoes found?
5 Which city is located close to the Po Delta?
6 Which is the longest river flowing into the Tyrrhenian Sea after the Tiber?

Look at the temperature and rainfall charts for three Italian towns and answer the following:

1 What is the climate of Cortina d'Ampezzo like in the summer? Why is there not much rainfall in the winter?
2 Why do you think Palermo is much drier than Milan?
3 How would you describe the winters in Palermo?
4 Which of these places has the biggest temperature range during the year?

Map legend:
- Land between 500 – 1000 metres
- Land over 1000 metres
- Old volcano
- Active volcano
- Lake

those which drain east to the Adriatic. The Tiber, which enters the sea near Rome, is the biggest of the Tyrrhenian rivers. In the extreme south and Sicily, rivers are little more than gravelly torrents which dry up completely during the summer months.

Climate

There is a lot of difference in climate between one part of Italy and another. The Alps have severe winters with heavy snowfall, but the summers are warm and wet. The Northern Plain has cold winters with long foggy periods, yet the summers are hot and dry, with occasional thunderstorms. The rest of Italy has a more typically *Mediterranean* climate with mild rainy winters and very hot, dry summers which leave the landscape parched and dusty.

Certain winds cause sudden changes in the weather. When the *scirocco* wind blows from the Sahara it brings muggy, hazy weather and sometimes rain containing desert dust. The *tramontana*, on the other hand, blows from the mountains and brings bright, fresh, clear conditions.

Temperature and rainfall charts

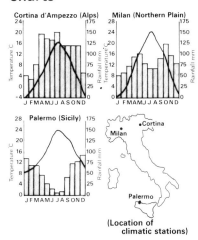

(Location of climatic stations)

2 The People of Italy

Italy is divided into twenty administrative regions or *regioni*, which vary in size and population. Many of them still have the ancient names the Romans gave them over two thousand years ago.

Regional differences

When the Roman Empire fell Italy split into many small states, and it was not until 1871 that they were all joined together again into one nation. So Italy is quite a young country and regional pride is strong. Most people think first of their region or town and see themselves as Calabrian or Sicilian, Milanese or Roman and so on, rather than as Italian. Until quite recently many parts of Italy were cut off from Rome by mountains or sea and this has helped regionalism to survive.

Within the country there are strong cultural differences—especially between the north and south. Northerners, descended from barbarian invaders from over the Alps, are generally taller and fairer than southerners. South Italians have the more Arabic features of their conquerors who came from the southern shores of the Mediterranean.

Some people have said that these differences influence attitudes to work; that northerners are hard-working, industrious people while southerners tend to take life more easily, and this is why the south is poor and undeveloped. But the south's comparative backwardness is due to its difficult environment rather than the attitude of its inhabitants.

Language

The main language of Italy is of course Italian, but there are groups speaking other languages in several parts of the country. German is the first language of Trentino–Alto Adige, near the Austrian border, while French is the main language spoken in the Valle d'Aosta and Western Piedmont. Dotted around the mountain areas of southern Italy there are small communities of Albanians and Greeks who sought refuge there during wars in their own countries.

The regions

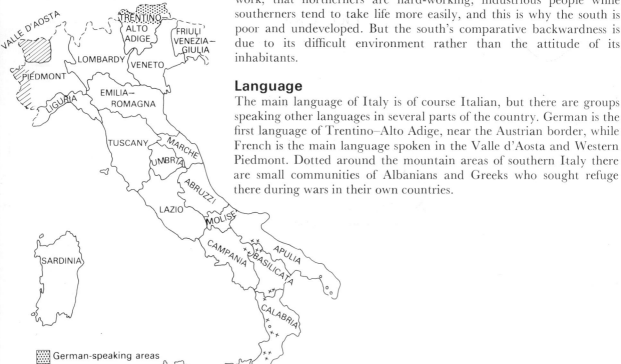

- ▦ German-speaking areas
- ▨ French-speaking areas
- × Albanian communities
- ○ Greek communities

0   100   200 km

Where people live

Italy's 56 million inhabitants live mostly in lowland areas. The biggest concentration of people is found in the Northern Plain which has both rich farmland and large industrial cities. Further south the coastal plains are heavily populated. By contrast, a relatively small number of people live in the mountain regions and the remote, barren interior of Sardinia.

Today most Italians are city dwellers and the towns are growing rapidly. Four cities—Rome, Milan, Naples and Turin—have over a million inhabitants and two others–Genoa and Palermo—could reach the million mark by the end of the century.

Population movement

Young people have for a long time been moving away from the poorer parts of Italy to find jobs elsewhere. Some go to the big industrial cities of the north while others leave the country altogether to work in Switzerland or West Germany, or even in the USA and Australia. They go in search of high wages and generally send back large sums of money to their relatives.

At the beginning of this century over ten million Italians left Italy to settle permanently in the USA, Argentina and elsewhere.

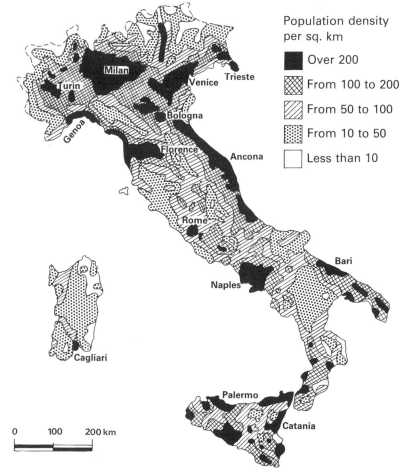

Population density per sq. km

■ Over 200
▨ From 100 to 200
▧ From 50 to 100
▒ From 10 to 50
□ Less than 10

0   100   200 km

Distribution of population

7

3 The Italian Economy

Italy was a founder member of the European Economic Community (EEC) which was formed in 1958 with the signing of the Treaty of Rome. The country has gained a lot from its membership: by exporting Mediterranean foodstuffs, importing iron and steel and receiving money from the Community's Regional Development Fund.

Italy is one of the poorest nations in the EEC mainly because of the difficulties it has had in developing the South. Indeed, Italy is like two nations: a heavily industrialized North which enjoys a high standard of living, and a poor, backward South which depends on agriculture.

Agriculture

About one in seven Italians works on the land. This figure is high for a developed Western country and gives a picture of southern Italy rather than of the north.

Northern Italian agriculture, especially in the Northern Plain, is commercial, efficient, highly mechanized and requires few farm workers. Large flat expanses are under wheat, maize, rice and sugar beet which can be easily harvested by machine. There is also a lot of rich pasture for dairy cattle and these provide milk and cheese for the big industrial cities. Even the hill country and Alpine valleys are intensely cultivated and their grapevines and other fruit crops produce rich harvests.

By contrast most of the south is mountainous. Its dry, rocky land is difficult to work and it is often more practical for farmers to do things

Traditional farmers working by hand in central Italy

by hand than use machines. The types of crop best suited to the southern climate are vines, olives, oranges and lemons, and vegetables, all of which require a lot of attention, especially at harvest time. There is little rich cattle pasture in the south, but plenty of rough grazing land for sheep on the hillsides where cultivation is impossible.

For centuries one of the main problems in the south was land ownership. Vast areas were owned by rich landowners who ran inefficient estate farms known as *latifondi*. The majority of the people remained landless peasants. This situation is gradually changing with land reform; the *latifondi* are being divided among the agricultural workers.

Energy

Italy has few energy sources of its own and is suffering more than most countries in the present energy crisis. It has supplies of natural gas but imports almost all its coal and oil. The country's great advantage is its mountains and a large amount of the power supply for industry can be produced cheaply as hydro-electricity. Power stations are plentiful in the Alps and most of their electricity is used in the Northern Plain. Hydro-electric power is also important in the Apennines.

Industry

With their large coal supplies, Britain, France and Germany all underwent rapid industrialization in the early 19th century. Italy, however, with only a few small coalfields, was a late industrial developer. It only began to industrialize in the 1860s when the country was being reunited, and most of its first factories were built in the Northern Plain. This was better suited than elsewhere because many people lived there, there was plenty of flat land, good road and river communications and export outlets through the ports of Genoa and Venice. The pattern has not changed much since then. The majority of Italian industry is still in the north, and Milan and Turin are the two most important centres of manufacturing. Many northern Italian firms are of international importance, including FIAT and Alfa-Romeo (cars), Pirelli (rubber products) and Olivetti (business machinery).

Coastal positions are becoming more and more important for large-scale industries such as iron and steel, chemicals and oil refining. There are huge modern developments taking place along the coast in such places as Ravenna and Porto Marghera–Mestre (Venice) where cheap, flat land is available.

New industry in the South: a chemical plant in Basilicata

La Cassa per il Mezzogiorno (The fund for the South)

The south of Italy is known as the *Mezzogiorno* (which means 'mid-day'). There are various ideas as to how it got this name, the most likely being that the sun is always higher in the sky here than it is further north.

The problems of the south had concerned the Italian government for a long time. In 1950 it set up a special fund *La Cassa per il Mezzogiorno*, which has since provided large sums of money for development schemes in the south.

Many improvements in farming methods have been made and the food production of the *Mezzogiorno* has greatly increased. The amount of

A new *superstrada* in Sicily

land under irrigation has gone up dramatically, land reform has taken place rapidly, and in many places unproductive marshlands have been drained to provide excellent farmland.

Industrial projects have also been encouraged. The *Cassa* has set up Italy's biggest steelworks at Taranto in Apulia and has helped the development of oil and chemical plants at various points along the Sicilian and Sardinian coasts.

Easy travel and transport are often the key to economic development and a great deal of the *Cassa* money has been spent on road improvements. New, fast, straight *autostrade* (motorways) and *superstrade* (super highways) are gradually replacing the narrow, winding old roads of the south.

The Mezzogiorno

Tourists in the Forum, Rome

Trade and tourism

Italy has long been a busy place for sea trade. Ports such as Genoa, Venice, Naples and Bari have for centuries handled goods from all round the Mediterranean and beyond. Through them come the country's main imports of oil, cereals, scrap metal and chemicals; out through them go exports of textiles, leather, wine, fruit and processed foods.

One of Italy's most important industries is tourism. With its warm climate, sandy beaches and clear seas, beautiful mountains and historic cities, Italy is one of Europe's most attractive tourist destinations and has over 10 million foreign visitors each year.

Regional autonomy

Valle d'Aosta, Trentino–Alto Adige, Friuli–Venezia Giulia, Sardinia and Sicily are five *regioni* which have a special status under Italian law. Known as 'autonomous regions' they are self-governing in such matters as planning, forestry, agriculture and tourism.

The three northern *regioni* have been granted autonomy mainly for political reasons. Valle d'Aosta and Trentino–Alto Adige have language minorities which have formed political separatist movements and Friuli–Venezia Giulia has frontier problems with Yugoslavia. Sicily and Sardinia, on the other hand, have severe economic problems resulting from their historical isolation from the mainland.

Autonomy, in theory, gives these regions much more say in their political affairs, enabling them to overcome their economic problems.

Questions

1. What do the letters EEC stand for? Who were the other five founder members?
2. Only 2 per cent of the working population of the USA and of Britain are involved in agriculture. How does this compare with Italy?
3. Why is agriculture backward in southern Italy?
4. What is land reform? How will it help farm workers in southern Italy?
5. Why is hydro-electricity so cheap to produce?
6. Look at the relief map of Italy in Chapter 1. In which parts of Sicily and Sardinia might hydro-electric plants be built?
7. How is a large number of people living in a small area an advantage for industrial development?
8. Look at the map of the *Mezzogiorno*. How many *regioni* receive money from the fund? Which *regione* is only partly in the *Mezzogiorno?* Can you suggest why the north of it is not? Roughly how much of the *Mezzogiorno* has been affected by land reform?
9. Easy travel and transport are often the key to economic development. Why?
10. Tourism is described as an 'invisible export'. Why do you think this is?

11

4 Piedmont and Valle d'Aosta

These two regions occupy the north-west corner of Italy. The Valle d'Aosta is completely Alpine, but Piedmont stretches from the Alps down to the Northern Plain. The very name Piedmont, (*Piemonte* in Italian) means 'foot of the mountain'.

Farming in Piedmont

Two of the major farm products of Piedmont are rice and wine. There is a large area given over to rice between the rivers Po and Ticino around the town of Vercelli (see maps below). The paddy fields look like those in China or India and farm workers used to wear large straw hats and wade knee deep in muddy water to plant the rice. Nowadays all the work is done by machine.

The hilly country around the town of Asti, known as *Monferrato* and *Langhe*, is covered with vineyards. Its soil is rich and the area produces some good quality wines. The most famous of these are *Asti Spumante*, a sparkling white wine said to be Italy's equivalent to Champagne, and *Barolo*, a rich fruity red wine.

Piedmont and Valle d'Aosta

France Switzerland

Chamonix
Gt. St. Bernard Pass
Cervino (4478)
M. Rosa (4633)
Monte Bianco (4807)
Courmayeur
Aosta
Lake Maggiore
Little St. Bernard Pass
R. Sesia
R. Dora Baltea
R. Ticino
Gran Paradiso (4061)
Novara
Vercelli
R. Dora Riparia
Turin
R. Po
MONFERRATO
Asti
Alessandria
R. Maira
R. Po
LANGHE
Cuneo
R. Gesso
M. Argentera (3297)

0 10 20 30 40 km

- Highland
- Permament snow and ice
- Paddy fields
- Limits of the Asti vineyard zone

The historic centre of Turin during the winter

Turin

With one and a quarter million people, Turin (Torino) is Italy's fourth largest city. It was founded as a Roman colony on the site of a Celtic village at the time of the Emperor Augustus. The present spacious, well-laid-out town centre dates from the last two centuries. As it was the royal capital of the kings of Piedmont–Sardinia, it became the first capital of the united Italy between 1861 and 1865 (see Chapter 45).

From the 1860s onwards Turin underwent rapid modernization and industrialization. Today it is second only to Milan as a centre of manufacturing, with textiles, metal-working and engineering as its main industries. Its most important single industry is FIAT (*Fabbrica Italiana Automobilistica Torino*) which was founded by Giovanni Agnelli in 1899. Today FIAT employs 180,000 people mainly in the Turin area but has factories throughout Italy. Many of Turin's other industries, such as steel-making and electrical engineering, are closely linked to the manufacture of motor vehicles.

Valle d'Aosta

This French-speaking area is Italy's smallest *regione*. The *valle* (valley) itself was formed by the Dora Baltea River as it carved its way through the Alps. In the north, two of the main Alpine peaks, Mont Blanc (*Monte Bianco*) and the Matterhorn (*Cervino*) form part of the boundary between Italy and its neighbours, France and Switzerland.

The valley forms part of many important routes and the town of Aosta was a major Roman fortress at the junction of various roads leading to the Alpine passes. Today it is still a route centre for traffic on its way to and from France and Switzerland. Cars cross the Alps over the two St Bernard Passes or through the 11km Mont Blanc Tunnel—one of the wonders of modern engineering. Aosta still has many Roman ruins in its historic centre, but has a thriving steelworks on its outskirts.

Valle d'Aosta is one of Italy's leading winter sports centres. On the higher slopes, skiing can take place all year round at such resorts as Cervinia.

FIAT factory

The highest part of the Italian Alps, Aosta

Questions

1 In what places do vines grow best?
2 Why do you think *Asti Spumante* is regarded as Italy's equivalent to Champagne?
3 Look at the map and say why you think Turin is in a good position.
4 What industries can you think of which are closely associated with motor car manufacturing?
5 How high are Mont Blanc and the Matterhorn?
6 Italy's highest mountain is on the border between Valle d'Aosta and Piedmont. What is it called?
7 Why was Aosta so important to the Romans?
8 What are the advantages of building a tunnel under Mont Blanc?

For further research

Find out how important FIAT is in relation to other motor car manufacturers. List the main motor car producers in the world, and the countries in which they started.

5 Liguria

Liguria forms a narrow arc along the sea, 250km long but only about 30km wide. It is bounded on the north by the Apennines and on the south by the Ligurian Sea. Most of the land is mountainous or hilly, and the only small patches of lowland are along the coast.

Farming

Less than a quarter of Liguria is farmland, and even this has been created by careful terracing of the lower slopes close to the coast. Plots of land are small and mainly grow fruit and vegetables. This gives the region a 'garden' appearance.

Liguria has a very pleasant climate. The influence of the sea gives it particularly mild winters during which the region is protected from northerly winds by the Apennines. Conditions are ideal for olives and citrus fruits (which are sensitive to frost) as well as for vines, apples, pears, peaches and flowers. Holiday villas line the coast and many exotic sub-tropical plants grow in their gardens.

Further inland the higher slopes are less productive. Much of the land is covered with beech and chestnut forest and the villages are rather run-down. Local people work in forestry or raise sheep and cattle.

Liguria

Genoa

Genoa (*Genova*) is Italy's first port. This is because it is the nearest port to Milan and Turin and is an outlet for the whole industrial area of the Northern Plain. Genoa's influence even stretches beyond Italy as it acts as Switzerland's outlet into the Mediterranean.

The city has a long history and was at the height of its power in the 13th century. It was a separate city state then and had colonies throughout the Mediterranean. One of its most famous sons was Christopher Colombus.

ino – Alto Adige

This region takes its name partly from the town of Trento and part
from the upper course (*alto* = high) of the River Adige. It is differe
from other parts of Italy because it is entirely mountainous and mai
of the people living there speak German. For a long time the regi
was part of the Austrian Empire, and it only became Italian in 191
Its people have a very strong sense of regional identity.

Mountain farming

Good land is scarce in Trentino–Alto Adige so most farmers depend
Alpine cattle. In the summer months the cattle are taken to feed on th
high pastures above the tree-line, at about 2000 metres. In th
autumn they are brought back, stage by stage, to the valleys. In th
middle of winter, when the villages are snowbound, they are kept
byres and fed on fodder crops. These include hay cut during th
summer from the high pastures. This system of farming is known
transhumance.

Trentino–Alto Adige

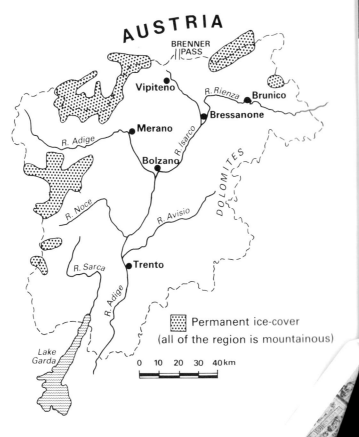

in an Alpine valley

The town of Genoa from the port

Hemmed in by mountains, Genoa looks like a jumble of old buildings and modern blocks of flats. The bustling port handles trade with
all parts of the world, and runs regular ferries to Sicily, Sardinia, Spain
and North Africa.

The city has developed a lot of heavy industry, including the massive
steelworks at Cornigliano.

The Italian Riviera

The Ligurian coastline, known as the Italian Riviera, is a continuation
of the French Riviera. It is one of the most beautiful stretches of coast
in Europe and has long been a summer resort centre. The wooded
mountains drop right down to the sea and small towns and fishing
villages have grown up where space permits. Portofino and Rapallo,
with their attractive colour-washed houses piled up behind their
harbours, are two of the popular older resorts which attracted visitors
from Northern Europe over a century ago.

Many modern resorts have been built along the coast in recent years
and are connected by a many-tunnelled railway and motorway.

Questions

1 Why does the land have to be
   terraced in Liguria?
2 Why is the climate of the region so
   mild in winter?
3 What sort of sub-tropical plants
   would you expect to see in villa
   gardens along the coast?
4 Look at a map of the Mediterranean in an atlas. To which
   Spanish port and to which town
   in Sicily do you think the ferries
   from Genoa go?
5 Why is Genoa Switzerland's
   Mediterranean outlet?
6 Do you know the names of any of
   the resorts on the French Riviera?
   List them from an atlas.
7 Why do the road and railway go
   through so many tunnels along the
   Ligurian coast?

The resort town of Portofino

6 Lombardy

Lombardy (*Lombardia*) is named after the Lombards who invaded the Po Valley and set up a kingdom there in the 6th century AD (see Chapter 39). Successful farming and industry in modern Lombardy make it the economic centre of Italy.

Mountains and lakes

The Alps stretch across northern Lombardy. There are several peaks over 3500 metres, and snow during both winter and summer makes skiing possible all year round in resorts such as Bormio.

The River Adda has cut a great valley through the mountains, known as the *Valtellina*. Its terraced south-facing slopes are covered with vineyards and orchards and these produce heavy crops of fruit.

At the foot of the Alps is a line of 'ribbon lakes' of which Lago Maggiore, Lago di Como and Lago di Garda are the largest. These were formed after the Ice Ages by *moraine* deposits which acted as natural dams across the river valleys. The lakes are popular summer tourist spots as well as favourite weekend resorts for the Milanese.

Farming on the plain

The Po Valley is Italy's 'bread basket' and Lombardy has the most productive part of it. The region produces more wheat and maize than any other. But not all the land is under cereals for this is also an important area for dairy produce. Canals help to drain away excess water from the fields in winter and to supply water for irrigation in summer. The landscape of the area is made up of flat, smallish fields surrounded by canals and rows of poplar trees.

A typical village on the Plain of Lombardy

Lombardy

[Map of Lombardy showing Bormio, Bernina (4049), Sondrio, VALTELLINA, ALPS, Lake Maggiore, Lake Como, Varese, Como, Lake of Iseo, Bergamo, Milan, Monza, Brescia, Lake Garda, R. Ticino, R. Lambro, R. Adda, R. Oglio, Pavia, Cremona, Mantua, R. Po, APENNINES]

Highland
0 10 20 30 40 km

Many people work in farming and live either in villag farms known as *cascine*. People in many of the smaller to Plain process the food produced in the surrounding countrysi

The textile industry

Lombardy has long been famous for the fine cloth made the woollen industry—originally based on the wool of m sheep—developed in the towns of the Alpine foothills and one of Bergamo, is still a major cloth producer.

Silk manufacture is concentrated in the area around Varese Como, and Varese is also a centre for the Lombard cotton industry keep up with modern developments, the cloth-producing towns of region are now increasing their output of synthetic fibres.

Milan

Milan (*Milano*) has a long history. Founded by the ancient Celts, came under Roman rule in 222 BC. Today it has over two million people and is Italy's second city.

Milan is well placed as a communications centre and has plenty of room for industrial growth. The development of hydro-electricity in the Alps and the discovery of natural gas in the Po Valley have allowed Milan to become Italy's main manufacturing city. It is also the commercial centre of Italy. The *Borsa* or stock-exchange, together with many bank and business headquarters, are located here rather than in Rome, the capital.

The inner city has high-rise office blocks which are beginning to overshadow the narrow Medieval streets and historic buildings such as the elaborate *Duomo* (cathedral). Milan is also important as an international centre of fashion and has Italy's most famous opera house, *La Scala*.

The smaller towns of Lombardy

Lombardy, like much of Italy, has historic towns and cities. Cremona, with its 13th-century cathedral, was once the home of Stradivarius, the violin maker, and is still a centre for the manufacture of musical instruments. Mantua (*Mantova*), is famous for its enormous Ducal Palace and bustling market squares. Pavia, once the ancient Lombard capital, has a covered bridge over the River Ticino and a short distance away, a magnificent *Certosa* or Charterhouse priory.

The *Certosa* of Pavia

7 Trent

o
fa
4 W
bei
5 Loo
fall
(page
are n
winter
6 Why
compar
cities?
7 The wo
'purse'. H
exchange
8 To which
tually lose i
Lombardy?
9 Look at the
Certosa of Pav
Milan. How
their architectu

For further rese

Look up Milan in e
find out more about
ings and way of life.

The town of Genoa from the port

Questions

1 Why does the land have to be terraced in Liguria?
2 Why is the climate of the region so mild in winter?
3 What sort of sub-tropical plants would you expect to see in villa gardens along the coast?
4 Look at a map of the Mediterranean in an atlas. To which Spanish port and to which town in Sicily do you think the ferries from Genoa go?
5 Why is Genoa Switzerland's Mediterranean outlet?
6 Do you know the names of any of the resorts on the French Riviera? List them from an atlas.
7 Why do the road and railway go through so many tunnels along the Ligurian coast?

The resort town of Portofino

   Hemmed in by mountains, Genoa looks like a jumble of old buildings and modern blocks of flats. The bustling port handles trade with all parts of the world, and runs regular ferries to Sicily, Sardinia, Spain and North Africa.

   The city has developed a lot of heavy industry, including the massive steelworks at Cornigliano.

The Italian Riviera

The Ligurian coastline, known as the Italian Riviera, is a continuation of the French Riviera. It is one of the most beautiful stretches of coast in Europe and has long been a summer resort centre. The wooded mountains drop right down to the sea and small towns and fishing villages have grown up where space permits. Portofino and Rapallo, with their attractive colour-washed houses piled up behind their harbours, are two of the popular older resorts which attracted visitors from Northern Europe over a century ago.

   Many modern resorts have been built along the coast in recent years and are connected by a many-tunnelled railway and motorway.

15

6 Lombardy

Lombardy (*Lombardia*) is named after the Lombards who invaded the Po Valley and set up a kingdom there in the 6th century AD (see Chapter 39). Successful farming and industry in modern Lombardy make it the economic centre of Italy.

Mountains and lakes

The Alps stretch across northern Lombardy. There are several peaks over 3500 metres, and snow during both winter and summer makes skiing possible all year round in resorts such as Bormio.

The River Adda has cut a great valley through the mountains, known as the *Valtellina*. Its terraced south-facing slopes are covered with vineyards and orchards and these produce heavy crops of fruit.

At the foot of the Alps is a line of 'ribbon lakes' of which Lago Maggiore, Lago di Como and Lago di Garda are the largest. These were formed after the Ice Ages by *moraine* deposits which acted as natural dams across the river valleys. The lakes are popular summer tourist spots as well as favourite weekend resorts for the Milanese.

Farming on the plain

The Po Valley is Italy's 'bread basket' and Lombardy has the most productive part of it. The region produces more wheat and maize than any other. But not all the land is under cereals for this is also an important area for dairy produce. Canals help to drain away excess water from the fields in winter and to supply water for irrigation in summer. The landscape of the area is made up of flat, smallish fields surrounded by canals and rows of poplar trees.

A typical village on the Plain of Lombardy

Lombardy

Many people work in farming and live either in villages or estate farms known as *cascine*. People in many of the smaller towns of the Plain process the food produced in the surrounding countryside.

The textile industry

Lombardy has long been famous for the fine cloth made there. The woollen industry—originally based on the wool of mountain sheep—developed in the towns of the Alpine foothills and one of them, Bergamo, is still a major cloth producer.

Silk manufacture is concentrated in the area around Varese and Como, and Varese is also a centre for the Lombard cotton industry. To keep up with modern developments, the cloth-producing towns of the region are now increasing their output of synthetic fibres.

Milan

Milan (*Milano*) has a long history. Founded by the ancient Celts, it came under Roman rule in 222 BC. Today it has over two million people and is Italy's second city.

Milan is well placed as a communications centre and has plenty of room for industrial growth. The development of hydro-electricity in the Alps and the discovery of natural gas in the Po Valley have allowed Milan to become Italy's main manufacturing city. It is also the commercial centre of Italy. The *Borsa* or stock-exchange, together with many bank and business headquarters, are located here rather than in Rome, the capital.

The inner city has high-rise office blocks which are beginning to overshadow the narrow Medieval streets and historic buildings such as the elaborate *Duomo* (cathedral). Milan is also important as an international centre of fashion and has Italy's most famous opera house, *La Scala*.

The smaller towns of Lombardy

Lombardy, like much of Italy, has historic towns and cities. Cremona, with its 13th-century cathedral, was once the home of Stradivarius, the violin maker, and is still a centre for the manufacture of musical instruments. Mantua (*Mantova*), is famous for its enormous Ducal Palace and bustling market squares. Pavia, once the ancient Lombard capital, has a covered bridge over the River Ticino and a short distance away, a magnificent *Certosa* or Charterhouse priory.

The *Certosa* of Pavia

The *Duomo* of Milan

Questions

1 What are the main attractions for tourists in the Lombardy Alps?
2 Why do you think the Lombardy lakes are known as ribbon lakes?
3 Why are the vineyards and orchards on the Valtellina's *south-facing* slopes?
4 What is meant by the Po Valley being Italy's 'bread basket'?
5 Look at the temperature and rainfall graph for Milan in Chapter 1 (page 5). Why do you think canals are needed for flood prevention in winter and irrigation in summer?
6 Why do you think some people compare Milan to American cities?
7 The word *borsa* is Italian for 'purse'. How do you think the stock exchange got its name?
8 To which city did Pavia eventually lose its position as capital of Lombardy?
9 Look at the photographs of the *Certosa* of Pavia and the *Duomo* of Milan. How would you describe their architecture?

For further research

Look up Milan in encyclopedias and find out more about its famous buildings and way of life.

7 Trentino – Alto Adige

This region takes its name partly from the town of Trento and partly from the upper course (*alto* = high) of the River Adige. It is different from other parts of Italy because it is entirely mountainous and many of the people living there speak German. For a long time the region was part of the Austrian Empire, and it only became Italian in 1919. Its people have a very strong sense of regional identity.

Mountain farming

Good land is scarce in Trentino–Alto Adige so most farmers depend on Alpine cattle. In the summer months the cattle are taken to feed on the high pastures above the tree-line, at about 2000 metres. In the autumn they are brought back, stage by stage, to the valleys. In the middle of winter, when the villages are snowbound, they are kept in byres and fed on fodder crops. These include hay cut during the summer from the high pastures. This system of farming is known as *transhumance*.

A village in an Alpine valley

Trentino—Alto Adige

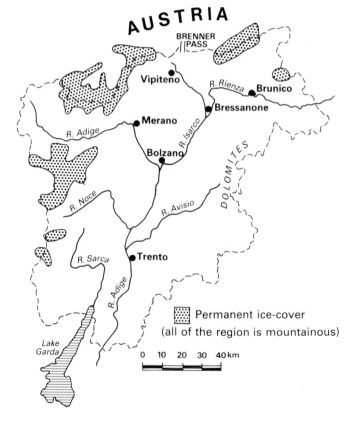

Not surprisingly, milk and butter are major products of this region. The more sheltered, sunny mountainsides, however, are terraced and covered with fruit trees and grape vines. The fruit ripens during the long warm summers.

Towns

Bolzano with its Gothic architecture, steep roofs and arcaded shops looks like an Austrian city. With cheap local hydro-electricity, it is a thriving centre for the metal and engineering industries. It is also the last main town before the Austrian border and is an important rail and road point on the way to the Brenner Pass.

Trento is much more Italian in character. Once famous as the place where the 'Council of Trent' was held (see Chapter 43), it is now a busy commercial centre.

The main road to Austria: the Brenner Pass *autostrada*

Tourism

Much of Trentino–Alto Adige's income is from tourism. Dozens of mountain resorts attract thousands of people each year, especially from the industrial cities of the Northern Plain and from the other side of the Austrian border, both of which are within easy reach.

Because the area is German-speaking and the cost of living in Italy is lower than in Austria or West Germany, the resorts are very attractive to people from these two countries. Towns such as Merano, Ortisei and Vipiteno are well-equipped with modern hotels, ski-lifts and other tourist facilities.

The Dolomites, which are on the eastern border of the region, are a centre during the summer for walking and rock climbing as well as a winter skiing area.

Questions

1 Which two factors have given the people of Trentino–Alto Adige a strong sense of regional identity, and why?
2 The system of *transhumance* is dying out in some parts of Europe because young people are unwilling to become involved in it. Why do you think this is?
3 Look at the temperature and rainfall chart in Chapter 1 (page 5) for Cortina d'Ampezzo (which is in the nearby Venetian Dolomites). Is it surprising that despite long, cold winters, apples, pears and grapes can thrive in an Alpine climate?
4 Why do buildings have steep roofs in Alpine areas?
5 Referring back to Chapter 3, why do you think the cost of living is lower in Italy than in Austria or West Germany?
6 Look at the photograph of the *autostrada* near the Brenner Pass. Why do you think it is raised in this way?
7 Look at the photograph of the ski-lift station in the Dolomites. What do you notice about the sign in the picture?

A ski-lift station in the Dolomites

8 Venetia

The north-east corner of Italy was dominated for centuries by the powerful maritime republic of Venice. It gives its name to two *regioni*—the *Veneto* and *Friuli Venezia-Giulia*— and together they form Venetia.

Venice

Venice (*Venezia*) is a unique city. Set in the middle of a shallow lagoon, it is built on hundreds of tiny islands. It was first settled over a thousand years ago by people from the mainland fleeing the invading barbarians. They hid in the marshes and reclaimed land upon which they built their homes. The water was a good natural defence.

The town, well positioned for trading, increased its wealth throughout the Middle Ages. It became a powerful independent state and gained control over the Eastern Alps and the Adriatic. After the 16th century it went into decline.

The superb marble palaces and churches of Venice are built on wooden piles driven deep into the mud of the lagoon. The weight of the buildings has caused the piles to sink and this is now a great problem. When there are high tides and storms at sea the squares and lower storeys of houses are flooded. Experts from all over the world are trying to find ways to step the buildings sinking any further and to prevent flooding.

There are no cars in Venice and the only way to get around the city is by boat or on foot. The main form of transport is the *motoscafo* or

A gondola on the Grand Canal

Venetia

motorboat, and there are regular 'bus' services of these boats along the canals. The *gondola*, which was once the most common type of boat in Venice, is now used for short taxi trips across the Grand Canal, or by tourists wanting to see the sights at a leisurely pace.

The Grand Canal, the high street of Venice, is crossed by three bridges. The most famous of these is the elegant Rialto, lined with shops. The heart of the city is *Piazza San Marco* (St Mark's Square) with the cathedral at one end and arcaded shops on the other three sides.

Tourism is old Venice's main source of income. Millions of visitors flock into the city throughout the year to look at its art and architectural treasures. Across the water is the new Venice. Mestre and Porto Marghera are new industrial settlements built on the mainland to keep Venice's economy alive. Many of the inhabitants of old Venice have moved there to find better houses and jobs. However, these industrial cities have added to old Venice's problems by polluting the lagoon.

The Po Delta

Just to the south of the Venetian Lagoon is the Po Delta. Its marshy land has gradually been drained to provide farmland. The fields are rectangular and surrounded by canals. Much of the land is below sea level, because it shrinks when it dries out, and sea walls have been built to prevent flooding.

Trieste

Close to the border with Yugoslavia is Trieste. It was Austrian for over a century and for a while was the Austrian Empire's main port. Together with the Istrian Peninsula it became part of Italy after World War 1. After World War 2, however, the Italian-speaking Istrian Peninsula was given to Yugoslavia. Trieste now suffers from being cut off from the territory it once served as a port and is very much a frontier town. This makes industrial development slow and has left Trieste an economic backwater.

Delivering beer by boat on a small canal in Venice

Venetian gondoliers in their distinctive costumes

Questions

1 What makes Venice so different from other cities?
2 What were the advantages to the early settlers of building a city in the marshes?
3 Why do you think that the *motoscafo* has widely replaced the *gondola*?
4 Look at the photograph of the gondoliers. What special outfit do they wear?
5 Can you think of any ways to stop the buildings in Venice sinking? How might you prevent Venice from being flooded from the sea? (Look at the map.)
6 What are the advantages and disadvantages of building new industrial towns on the edge of the Venetian lagoon?
7 From the map measure roughly how far the Po Delta projects out into the sea.
8 In what ways do you think the people of Trieste feel isolated from the rest of Italy?

For further research

Read as widely as you can about Old Venice; its buildings (especially St Mark's Basilica and the Doge's Palace); its glass industry; and the problems and pleasures of living in a city without roads.

21

9 Emilia – Romagna

Emilia–Romagna, partly in the Po Valley and partly in the Northern Apennines, stretches across almost the entire width of Italy. The Emilian Way, an ancient Roman road, runs through the region and links many of its most important towns.

Farming on the plain

Farming in Emilia–Romagna is highly mechanized. On the plain, rich soils and plenty of water mean that the land is well used. Wheat, sugar-beet and orchard crops are the main produce together with milk and cheese from rich dairy herds.

The landscape often has a regular appearance and some still shows the ancient pattern of *centuriation*. This dates back to Roman times when, as the plain was reclaimed, plots of land of a standard size were given to veteran soldiers in payment for their services.

Reclamation is still taking place in the marshlands to the east of the plain. The large lake of the *Valli di Comacchio* is gradually being drained and turned into farmland.

The Adriatic coast

Emilia–Romagna attracts hundreds of thousands of tourists during the summer months. The Adriatic has long sandy beaches and hotels and blocks of holiday flats line the coast from Cervia to Cattolica. Rimini, with 120,000 inhabitants, is the biggest resort and has a seasonal airport through which visitors flood from all over Europe.

San Marino

Many holidaymakers visiting Rimini go to San Marino for a day trip. This tiny city, perched on a series of rocky peaks and with less than

The Republic of San Marino

Emilia–Romagna

20,000 inhabitants, is not part of Italy. It is a separate republic. It became independent during the Middle Ages and is ruled over by a 'Grand Council' and two elected 'Captains Regent'. Its main source of income is from tourism and the minting of vast numbers of commemorative postage stamps.

Ravenna

Ravenna has a rich history and many fine buildings dating from the Byzantine period (see Chapter 39).

Natural gas has been discovered nearby and a new industrial complex based on it has recently been developed between the city and the sea. Ravenna's port, Porto Corsini, is one of Italy's biggest oil terminals.

Towns of the Emilian Way

The Emilian Way was opened in 187 BC and a number of Roman towns grew up along it. Bologna, with half a million people, is the capital of Emilia–Romagna and the largest of the Emilian Way towns. It has a famous university and takes pride in its well-preserved historic centre. Now heavily industrialized, Bologna specializes in food processing and engineering.

Parma is the centre of an important agricultural area and gives its name to a type of ham and *parmigiano* (parmesan) cheese. Modena is a centre of the car industry and both Maserati and Ferrari and based there.

The leaning towers at the centre of Bologna

The historic centre of Ferrara

Questions

1 What are the most important agricultural products of the region?
2 Why were ancient Romans given plots of land in Emilia-Romagna?
3 Look at the map of the region. What is it about the Emilian Way that tells you it was constructed by the Romans? Do you know the names of any other famous Roman roads?
4 What makes the Adriatic coastline so popular in summer? Why is Rimini airport seasonal?
5 When was the Byzantine period? Where was Byzantium?
6 Which major towns of the region are not on the Emilian Way?
7 The Po forms the border between Emilia-Romagna and which two other regions?
8 Apart from Maserati and Ferrari can you name four other Italian motor vehicle manufacturers?

10 Tuscany and Umbria

Tuscany (*Toscana*) and Umbria form a continuous geographical area. Their beautiful hill country has inspired many artists and their historic towns receive millions of tourists each year.

The hill country

The western parts of Tuscany and much of Umbria have a rolling landscape of cone-shaped hills. Their tops are wooded and the sides are terraced. Olives, vines and fruit trees are common, and grain is grown in the valleys and in some of the olive groves. In some of the more fertile places sunflowers and the bright green leaves of tobacco plants give extra colour to the countryside. Towns and villages are built in defensive positions on the hillsides.

The Tuscan hill country is very important for its wine, particularly for the full-bodied red *Chianti*. In some places, however, where the rocks are soft, erosion has left the land bare of vegetation and useless for agriculture.

Most of Umbria is farmed and there are few signs of heavy industry. The Nera Valley around the steelworks town of Terni is an exception.

Assisi, the birthplace of St Francis (see Chapter 50), is Umbria's most visited town and has a stream of pilgrims throughout the year.

Umbrian landscape near Assisi

Tuscany and Umbria

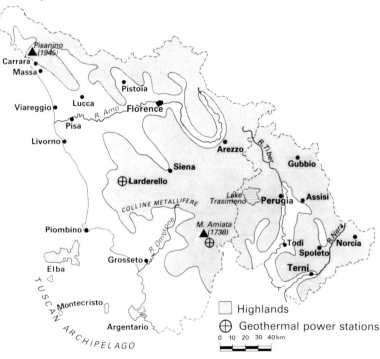

Many of the region's other small historical cities are equally interesting—including Todi, Norcia, Narni and Spoleto, which has one of Italy's biggest summer music festivals.

The Tuscan coastline

The northern and southern parts of the Tuscan coast are very different. In the north it is highly developed—long stretches of sandy beach have given rise to seaside resorts of which Viareggio is the most popular. Nearby are the two ports of Pisa and Livorno. Pisa, with its famous leaning tower, is on the River Arno and grew up as a trading centre and river port. It became powerful during the Middle Ages because of its commercial wealth. When the mouth of the Arno silted up, however, it lost its wealth and power but was given new life last century with the opening of the railways.

Livorno (sometimes known as Leghorn in English) is on the coast and therefore has many advantages over Pisa. It is a thriving modern port and has ship-building and oil refineries as well as Italy's Naval Academy.

The southern part of the Tuscan coast, the *Maremma*, is sparsely populated. Long stretches are lined with lagoons, sand bars and pinewoods. For centuries it was a hostile territory with swamps, malaria and brigands—so much so that it inspired part of the poet Dante's *Inferno* (see Chapter 52).

Now malaria has been wiped out, but farming remains relatively unmechanized and development is slow. One special feature of the Maremma is the white long-horned cattle which are still used for ploughing and pulling carts.

Questions

1 What are sunflowers used for?
2 Look at the photograph of the hill country. How would you describe it?
3 Why would Tuscany make a good centre for a varied holiday?
4 Look at Livorno and Pisa on the map. How would you describe their locations?
5 Do you think the Maremma is a good place to have nature reserves?
6 Look at the photograph of the cart drawn by Maremma cattle. Why have their horns been cut off?
7 Look at the position of Florence. Why do you think the River Arno rose so suddenly during 1966?
8 Look at the photograph of the *geothermal* power station. How would you describe the landscape?
9 Do you know of any other countries which produce electricity in this way?

A cart drawn by Maremma cattle

A general view of Florence and the River Arno

For further research

1 Find out more about *geothermal* energy, how it is produced, where it can be produced and what advantages it has over coal or oil-fired thermal energy.
2 From reference books, make a list of the various artists who were born in Tuscany and Umbria. Select two and study paintings they made showing the hill country in Tuscany and Umbria.

A geothermal power station in Tuscany

Florence

Florence (*Firenze*) is the regional capital of Tuscany. Set on the banks of the River Arno and surrounded by hills it is regarded by many as Italy's finest city. Millions of people arrive each year to see its buildings and works of art. Florence has Italy's two largest art galleries, the *Uffizi* and the *Pitti*.

The Arno behaves rather like a mountain torrent and in November 1966 after heavy rain it rose quickly, burst its banks and flooded the city. Countless art treasures were destroyed and structural damage was done to various buildings, including the city's quaint covered bridge, the *Ponte Vecchio*.

Today, Florence is a thriving industrial city with modern developments well away from the old buildings of the city centre.

Minerals and energy resources

The Etruscans (see Chapter 35) were attracted to Tuscany for its minerals, and the region still has many mines and quarries. There are mines providing Italy with three-quarters of its supply of iron on the island of Elba and near Grosseto. The biggest steelworks in Tuscany is at Piombino, the mainland port for Elba. In the *Colline Metallifere* (literally 'metal bearing hills'), zinc, lead and manganese are mined.

In the north of Tuscany are the great marble quarries of Carrara. First worked by the Romans, they were a favourite source of marble for Michelangelo (see Chapter 54).

In two places of former volcanic activity, Larderello and Monte Amiata, *geothermal* power is produced. Natural steam coming out of the ground is used to generate electricity. Great shining metal pipes run across the steaming countryside to the power stations.

11 Lazio

Lazio, ancient *Latium*, takes its name from the Latin peoples who lived there over three thousand years ago and later became the Romans. It is a region of contrasts—limestone mountains, volcanic hills and reclaimed coastal marshes. The region's capital is Rome (*Roma*).

Volcanic hill-country

Lazio has a chain of four extinct volcanoes. These were active between 25 million and 2 million years ago and then blew themselves apart to form huge craters, known as *calderas*. These craters then filled with water and formed the Lakes Bracciano, Vico, Bolsena, Albano and Nemi.

When active, these volcanoes were highly eruptive and scattered their ash over hundreds of square kilometres. This ash has now broken down into fertile soil which allows intensive farming, particularly of grapes for wine. The best known wines of Lazio are those of Frascati in the Alban Hills and Montefiascone on the slopes of Lake Bolsena's crater. Around Lake Vico, the hillsides are covered with hazel groves which produce nuts for the confectionery industry.

The small rivers of northern Lazio have carved out great gorges in the *tuffs* (rocks formed from volcanic ash). Between the gorges are easily defended sites ideal for settlement. Most of the small towns of the area are perched high on rocky outcrops overlooking deep wooded valleys.

Lazio

Extinct volcano

Crater lakes

Other highlands

0 10 20 30 40 km

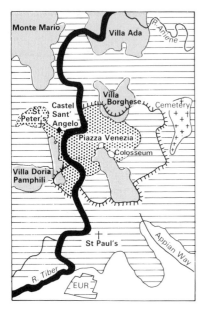

Modern Rome

Rome: the Spanish Steps

Vitorchiano, a village in Northern Lazio built on a volcanic plateau

Rome

The Tiber is the largest river on Italy's west coast. About 30km from the sea there is a small island which made a good bridging point in early times. Nearby were seven small volcanic hills. This was the original site of Rome. (See Chapters 36 and 37 for its early history.)

Italy's capital now has three million inhabitants and much of it is a lively modern city. The central core remains almost untouched by 20th-century development, but elsewhere multi-storey blocks of flats are common. Rome has all the problems of a modern city—traffic jams, not enough public transport, and pollution, which is eating into the marble of old statues, church fronts and the columns of ancient temples.

Rome is the centre of Italian government and the headquarters of the Food and Agricultural Organization of the United Nations. It is not a manufacturing town like Milan but relies on the production of luxury goods, the film industry and, above all, tourism.

Rome has two major groups of tourist attractions—its ancient archaeological, or classical, remains dating back as far as the 6th century BC, and its later Christian sites. The most spectacular classical monuments are the Forum and the Colosseum (see Chapters 36 and 37).

When Rome was rebuilt in the Baroque period, between 1500 and 1650, numerous new churches, such as the present St Peter's, were built. Many new *piazze* (squares), fountains, palaces and the elegant 'Spanish Steps' were also built at this time. It is these buildings that have made Rome into a gracious and attractive city.

In the midst of all this is 'Old Rome'—still basically medieval in character with a complicated tangle of narrow, winding streets.

Since 1871, when Rome became the capital of Italy, rapid building has taken place, but large areas of green open space remain within the city. These were the former villa estates of the nobility and are now public parks. In the south of Rome is E.U.R. (*Esposizione Universale di Roma*), a spacious garden city which was planned by Mussolini and completed recently.

The Vatican City

In the centre of Rome is an independent country, the Vatican City State. It is only half a square kilometre in area and has a resident population of about 1000 people, but is of world importance as the headquarters of the Roman Catholic Church.

The state was set up in 1929 (see Chapter 47) and is ruled over by the Pope. His sovereign territory includes St Peter's Basilica and Square, the Papal Palace, the Vatican Museums and gardens, as well as various administrative offices.

The Vatican City has many features of much larger states. It produces its own stamps and coins, it has a radio station which broadcasts world-wide, it publishes a daily newspaper, the *Osservatore Romano*, and even has its own railway station linking it to the main Italian rail network. The Vatican is said to be a very rich state but much of its wealth is tied up in its art treasures.

Rome: the River Tiber and the dome of St Peter's

The Pontine Marshes

In the south of Lazio between the Apennines and the sea is a large stretch of flat land known as the *Agro Pontino*. Until this century it was a hostile, malaria-infested swamp inhabited only by rough, semi-nomadic shepherds and their flocks.

It was reclaimed under Mussolini (see Chapter 47) between 1928 and 1932. Canals were dug to drain the land, new farms were established and shelter belts of fast-growing eucalyptus trees were planted to stop soil erosion. In 1932 the new town of Latina was built to act as a service centre for the farming district.

Questions

1 Why do you think the volcanic lakes of Bracciano, Bolsena, Vico, Albano and Nemi are circular?

2 Why do you think the small towns of northern Lazio could be easily defended?

3 Look at the photograph of Vitorchiano. How would you describe its setting and appearance?

4 Why was the island on the Tiber a good bridging point in ancient times?

5 What are the main tourist attractions in Rome?

6 Look at the map of Rome. What proportion of the city is medieval? How can you tell that the Tiber is close to the sea?

7 If Rome is not an industrial city, what causes the pollution?

8 Why were the Pontine Marshes so difficult to drain before the 20th century?

9 From which country do eucalyptus trees come? What advantage would they have in the Italian climate?

10 The wealth of the Vatican City is bound up in its art treasures. Why is this a disadvantage in practical terms?

For further research

Find out more about the city of Rome, its famous buildings and its development.

12 Marche, Abruzzi and Molise

These three regions stretch from the central Adriatic coastline to the highest parts of the Apennines, and have many similarities in their landscapes and economies.

The Adriatic coast

The greatest number of people in these mountainous regions live along the narrow, low-lying coastal strip which is lined with ports and seaside resorts. The ports are built on rocky promontories and at river mouths, while the holiday resorts are in the broad, open sandy bays.

Fishing is a major industry along the Adriatic coast, especially at San Benedetto del Tronto, Ancona, Pescara and Termoli. One big recent change is the appearance of off-shore prospecting rigs in search of oil and natural gas.

The Central Apennines

The highest part of the Apennine chain is formed mainly of limestone and has high, jagged peaks which are as dramatic as the Alps. In the

A crowded Adriatic beach at Termoli, Molise

Marche, Abruzzi and Molise

Abruzzi stands the *Gran Sasso d'Italia* with its series of rocky summits. The *Corno Grande* (meaning 'big horn') at 2912m is the highest and even has a small glacier on its northern face. The Gran Sasso area is important both for skiing in winter and walking and rock-climbing in the summer.

Nearby, in slightly lower but more heavily wooded mountain country, is the Abruzzi National Park. This was created to preserve endangered species of local wildlife, including bears, wolves, deer and wild goats.

Farming is restricted in these highlands and sheep rearing is common. Transhumance (see Chapter 7) is practised, with the grassy slopes above the tree-line being used for summer pasture.

The mountain basins

Within the central Apennines there are many *intermontane basins*: former lakes which have been choked with earth and rocks brought down by mountain streams. The soils are generally rich here and the broad depressions are a good sheltered setting for towns and villages. L'Aquila and Sulmona, two of the main Abruzzi towns, are set in such basins.

Further west is Fucino Basin (Conca del Fucino), which was still a lake until the mid-19th century when it was drained by digging tunnels through the mountains to a neighbouring river. Fucino has good farmland, much of which is planted with sugar beet.

Towns

Ancona is the main port of the central Adriatic and has a fishing fleet, shipbuilding yards, a container terminal and regular ferries to Yugoslavia, Greece and Israel. Built on a rocky headland, it was badly damaged by an earthquake in 1972.

Urbino, set in the rolling hills of Marche, is a major art centre and has a fine Ducal Palace. Further south is Ascoli Piceno, which grew up as a market town on the Via Salaria, the old 'salt road' that went from Rome to the salt pans of the Adriatic. L'Aquila, set high up in a mountain basin, is famous for its food products—particularly pork, lamb and cheeses. It has a massive Spanish castle, a reminder of centuries of foreign domination of the Abruzzo.

The port of Ancona

The Corno Grande, highest peak of the Apennines

Questions

1 What are the advantages of having a port on land jutting out into the sea or at the mouth of a river?
2 How does the height of the Corno Grande compare with the main peaks in the Alps?
3 Why do you think a glacier has formed on its *north-facing* slope?
4 Italy has been slow in developing its national parks. How many can you think of in your country? What are the advantages of having national parks?
5 Why are soils rich in *intermontane basins?*
6 What might Lake Fucino have been used for had it not been drained?
7 Why is there a castle built by the *Spanish* at L'Aquila?

For further research

Find out the origin of the word 'salary'. What has it to do with the *Via Salaria*? Find out how sea-salt is produced.

13 Campania

Campania is Latin for 'countryside' and the Romans gave the Naples region this name because it was such a productive farming area. It is a small but densely populated region with most people living around the Bay of Naples itself.

Vesuvius

The twin-peaked summit of the volcano Vesuvius can be seen from most places in the Bay of Naples and from a long way out to sea. One peak is the crater, quiet since 1944 but liable to erupt at any moment. The other is Monte Somma, a reminder of a once much greater mountain which blew itself to pieces in AD 79 destroying the towns of Herculaneum and Pompeii. Visitors to those two archaeological sites can see just how catastrophic the eruption was. On the edges of the excavated area are great walls of volcanic ash and solidified mud, well above head height.

Ischia and Capri

These two contrasting holiday islands are inside the Bay of Naples. Ischia is made of brown volcanic rocks and its wooded mountains tower above the many small villages and well-tended vineyards. Capri

Vesuvius and Herculaneum

Campania

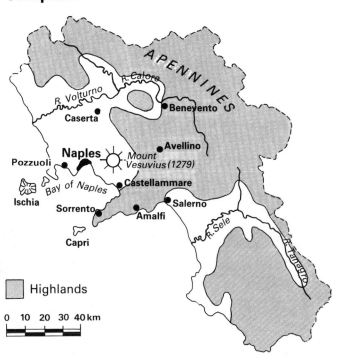

is much smaller and made of glistening white limestone, with huge cliffs rising sheer from the sea. It has two main towns and is dotted about with whitewashed villas set in gardens of lush sub-tropical vegetation. Both islands get very crowded at the height of the summer tourist season.

Farming in Campania

The eastern part of Campania is mountainous with poor rocky soils. Farms are not very productive here. The coastal zone is very different. The Bay of Naples has rich soils, formed from the ash and lava of Vesuvius, and is intensely cropped with fruits and vegetables.

Campania is the leading region in Italy for tomatoes, apricots, peaches, cherries and walnuts, and is also a major producer of grapes, citrus fruits and olives. Along the Sorrento Peninsula, in sheltered valleys and terraces under the cliff faces, are densely packed lemon groves. To the north of Naples the flat coastal plain is grazed by water buffalo whose milk is used to produce the special soft *mozzarella* cheese.

Naples

Naples (*Napoli*) is a gigantic, sprawling city, a mixture of beauty and squalor, and is one of Italy's liveliest and most exciting places. Its setting gives it one of the best harbours in the Mediterranean and throughout history it has been able to develop trade links with the rest of the world.

For hundreds of years, Naples was the capital of much of southern Italy which was ruled over by foreign monarchs. The elegant castle and royal palace complex in the centre of the city overlooks the sea.

The poor of Naples live in the old medieval quarter, known as *Spaccanapoli*. This area is teeming with life and full of rows of washing hanging across the narrow streets. Petty crime thrives in this area. In the more exclusive parts of the city there are luxurious villas set in well planted gardens. The difference between rich and poor is probably more noticeable in Naples than any other Italian city.

The port still accounts for much of Naples' income, with cargo vessels and passenger ships going to most parts of the world. The main traditional industry is food processing, with tomato canning and pasta manufacture especially important. On the fringes of the city are heavy industries, such as steelworks and oil refineries.

The harbour, Capri

The centre of Naples

Questions

1 Look at the photograph of Vesuvius and Herculaneum. What do you notice about the level of the modern buildings? What time of year do you think the picture was taken? (Vesuvius is 1279 metres high.)
2 Herculaneum and Pompeii are better preserved than many Roman towns. Why do you think this is?
3 How has geology influenced the character of the two islands of Ischia and Capri?
4 What makes such a small region as Campania so good for growing fruit and vegetables?
5 What might you see in fields around Naples which is more commonly seen in India?
6 Look at the map of Campania. What gives Naples such a fine position?
7 Look at a map of the Mediterranean in an atlas. With which other Mediterranean ports do you think Naples could have trading links?
8 Why are the heavy industries on the outskirts of Naples?

For further research

Find out more about volcanoes. *Vesuvian* is one of several types of volcano in a scale based upon the violence of their eruption. Find out what the other types are and where Vesuvius comes in the scale. Look up in history books the story of the destruction of Herculaneum and Pompeii.

14 Apulia

Apulia (*Puglia*) is set in the 'heel' of Italy and is a region of low hills and gently rolling plains. It is made almost entirely of limestone and water is scarce.

The water problem

There is usually little surface water in limestone areas. Apulia has a few small rivers in the north but elsewhere all water runs underground. To make matters worse, the region's rainfall is well below the national average.

Farmers have long been dependent upon well-water for their crops but this is not always reliable. Between 1902 and 1939 the *Acquedotto Pugliese* (Apulian Aqueduct) was built to bring water from wetter neighbouring *regioni* and to distribute it throughout Apulia. The main aqueduct is linked to an ever-growing network of smaller ones which are paid for by the *Cassa per il Mezzogiorno* (see Chapter 3).

Farming in Apulia

Apulia is intensely farmed and has little uncultivated land. More wine and olive oil is produced here than anywhere else in Italy. Almonds are also important and in some places are grown in mixed groves with olives.

The hilly *Murge* area has thin stony soils and the fields are painstakingly prepared for cultivation by collecting up the larger stones and putting them in piles. The plain of the *Tavoliere*, near Foggia, has richer soil, much of which is devoted to wheat. This wheat is the 'hard'

For further research

Find out more about limestone. How does water get underground in limestone areas and what features does it produce? Which parts of your country are made of limestone? Do they have the same sort of water problems as Apulia?

Ostuni, a *città contadina*

Apulia

variety, *grano duro*, which is used to make *pasta* rather than bread. The Salentine Peninsula is one of the few parts of Italy to specialize in tobacco, which is blended with the better imported varieties before being made into cigarettes.

Rural settlement

Throughout southern Italy, farmers and farmworkers tend to live in large villages. In parts of Apulia these villages may have as many as twenty or thirty thousand people living in them and are known as *città contadine* ('peasant cities'). They may be the size of a town but they keep the character of a village.

Inland from Bari, villages and farmhouses are built in a curious architectural style. The origin of these beehive-shaped houses, known as *trulli*, is believed to be prehistoric.

Gargano

The Gargano Peninsula is like a huge rocky limestone spur sticking out into the Adriatic. In recent years it has made a lot of money from tourism. Its deep, clear water has particularly attracted sub-aqua divers and fishermen, as have the tiny Tremiti islands 20km from the coast.

Towns

Apulia has a string of Adriatic coastal towns, the largest of which are Bari and Brindisi. Bari has a fine medieval core with a jumble of narrow streets inside the ancient city walls, and a well planned modern area with wide streets lined with palm trees. In the port area there is a lot of new industry.

Brindisi is a port at the end of the old Appian Way and, just as in Roman times, it is Italy's main crossing point for Greece. Outside the city is a vast petro-chemical industrial area using imported oil from the Middle East.

***Trulli* at Alberobello**

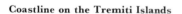

Questions

1 Why do limestone areas have water problems?
2 Look at an atlas, and decide which neighbouring regions you think may be wetter? (Think of the importance of highlands.)
3 Why do you think so much of Apulia is cultivated?
4 Look at the photograph of the *città contadina*. How would you describe its appearance?
5 Do sub-aqua divers prefer rocky or sandy coastlines? Why do you think Gargano is so popular with divers?
6 Look at the photograph of the Tremiti coastline. How would you describe it?
7 Which road did the ancient Romans take on their way to Greece?

Coastline on the Tremiti Islands

The city centre of Bari

15 Basilicata and Calabria

The southern-most part of the Italian peninsula is backward and poor compared with regions further north and many people leave because it is difficult to make a living from the land.

The hill-country of Basilicata

Inland from the Ionian Sea is a series of hill ranges which are cut through by four major rivers. These graved-filled *fiumare* have little water in them for most of the year. The hills are made of soft clays and mudstones and are deeply cut by erosion gullies. In the summer heat the soil is rock-hard and in the winter whole hillsides may be removed by violent storms. This erosion has been common ever since the ancient Romans cut down all the trees on the hillsides to build their ships.

Large villages were built on the hilltops because until a few decades ago malaria was common in the *fiumara* valleys. Farming has been slow to develop and donkeys are still widely used for carrying loads.

Improvements are gradually being made as the river valleys and coastal plain are reclaimed and irrigated and new farms are built there. As yet only a few people have been moved to lowland farms and many young people still leave the region every year. This in turn leads to villages being semi-abandoned and a further decline in the way of life of the area.

The old town of Matera

Basilicata and Calabria

The Earthquake of 1980

Much of Northern Basilicata was badly affected by an earthquake in the autumn of 1980. November 23rd had been an unusually warm day for that time of year throughout Italy. At 7.35 in the evening the earth shook and buildings collapsed in dozens of villages in the Potenza province of Basilicata and neighbouring Campania. Three thousand people lost their lives and hundreds of thousands were made homeless. Relief work was quick but often chaotic and was hampered by a sudden change in the weather—biting cold winds, heavy rainfall and snow. Some of the worst hit villages were completely abandoned and people rehoused elsewhere. In other villages reconstruction work started immediately, but tents and caravans could become a permanent feature of parts of the earthquake area.

The Sila Massif

In the centre of Calabria is a roughly circular granite upland known as the Sila. The area is thickly wooded (its name comes from the Latin *silva* meaning forest), and is snow-covered for much of the winter. Once charcoal burners and shepherds were the only people who lived there, and they only stayed during the summer.

Since 1950 the area has changed. Parts of the forest have been cleared and Alpine cattle introduced. But the biggest boost of all has come through tourism—especially for winter sports.

Towns

Most of the large towns in these two regions have grown rapidly in recent years and have a modern appearance. Reggio di Calabria, for example, was destroyed by an earthquake in 1908 and has since been completely rebuilt. Matera, however, is built on the side of a deep ravine and until quite recently many of its inhabitants lived in caves. Much of the old town is now being abandoned as erosion causes it gradually to crumble over the edge of the ravine.

High up in the Sila Massif, Calabria

1980 earthquake damage, Pescopagano, Basilicata.

Questions

1 Can you think of four different things mentioned in this chapter which suggest that Basilicata and Calabria are poor *regioni*?
2 What physical factors of the region could have made earthquake relief chaotic?
3 Why would some of the villages affected by the earthquake have been abandoned?
4 Why would Alpine breeds of cattle have been introduced to the Sila?
5 Look at the photograph of Matera. How would you describe its appearance?
6 Why does cutting down trees on a hillside speed up the process of soil erosion?

For further research

Find out more about earthquakes. In which parts of the world are earthquakes most likely to happen, and why?

16 Sicily

Sicily (*Sicilia*) is the largest island in the Mediterranean Sea and the most southerly of Italy's regions.

The Plain of Catania

Sicily is mainly mountainous but has a few coastal plains, the biggest of which surrounds the town of Catania. Rising above Catania is the volcano Etna, with its plume of smoke and a snow-cap in winter. Etna erupts frequently, damaging both crops and villages on its slopes. But people still live there because the volcanic soils are so fertile. The plain itself also has rich farmland which produces excellent oranges, lemons, olives, grapes and peaches.

Catania, a city of almost half a million people, is on the northern side of the plain. It was destroyed by an earthquake in 1693 and rebuilt with many fine, ornate buildings. At the southern end of the plain is the town of Augusta. It has a massive oil terminal and petrochemical works and is Sicily's largest industrial complex.

The interior of Sicily

The Sicilian interior is one of Italy's problem areas. Many people live there although it is a mountainous zone with poor soils. The Sicilians live mostly in overgrown villages high on the mountainsides. Farmers have always travelled long distances to their fields below. Much of the farmland is terraced hillside which produces a meagre harvest of grain, grapes, olives and vegetables.

The interior of Sicily, near Enna

Sicily

There is little work in towns such as Caltanisetta and Enna so many people leave to find jobs elsewhere. Discontent amongst local people is sharpened by the system of land ownership on the island. The land is mostly divided up into *latifondi* (large estates) which are owned by a few powerful families. This has always been a difficult local issue and one of the factors leading to the formation of outlawed organizations such as the Mafia (see Chapter 49).

The fishing industry

Sicily catches more fish than any other region of Italy because of its position inside the Mediterranean fishing grounds. It specializes in tuna and swordfish.

Tuna, the largest fish of the Mediterranean, are caught off the western coast and the Egadi Islands. It is a seasonal catch and done by surrounding the fish with nets and then harpooning them. Favignana Island has a large tuna canning factory. Swordfish are caught off the Straits of Messina and the Aeolian Islands. For this there are special boats with tall masts from which a look-out is kept. The fish are harpooned from a long walk-way projecting from the boat's prow.

Palermo

Palermo was ruled by the Arabs for two hundred years and its architecture has an oriental flavour. Close to the city centre is a network of narrow market streets just like an Arab bazaar.

Palermo is a city of contrasts. It has wide, elegant streets and squalid shanty towns, old craft workshops and modern industrial estates. The busy harbour, which handles freight and regular ferry services to Naples, Tunis and Sardinia, is one of the most beautiful in Italy.

The Aeolian Islands

These islands are volcanic and two of them are still active. Stromboli is a dark, sombre cone-shaped island. Its crater is in constant eruption and sends up fire bombs many times a day. Vulcano has not erupted since late last century, and it is uncertain when it will do so again. The long time-lapse means that the next eruption could be violent.

Landing swordfish at Messina

The sombre outline of the volcanic island of Stromboli

Questions

1 Why is the Plain of Catania better farmland than the Sicilian interior?
2 Why do you think villages in the Sicilian interior were built high on the mountainsides?
3 Look at the photograph of the swordfish being landed. How much would you say these fish weigh?
4 Why do you think swordfish and tuna are harpooned?
5 Why do you think Stromboli's frequent eruptions can be regarded as a 'safety valve'? Why might Vulcano's next eruption be violent?

For further research

Find out more about the fishing industry. Find out which has richer fishing grounds, the Atlantic or the Mediterranean, and why. Make a list of types of fish which are found in the Mediterranean but not in the Atlantic.

39

17 Sardinia

Cut off from mainland Italy by over 200km of sea, the island of Sardinia (*Sardegna*) has its own distinctive character.

The interior

The rough, windswept interior of Sardinia is made of hard ancient rocks, such as granite, which form a mixture of plateaux and peaks. The highest point in the Gennargentu mountains is just over 1800 metres. Much of the land is wood or scrub and few people live there. Villages are small and far apart, and roads and railways take winding routes over difficult terrain.

The major activity of the interior is sheep and goat rearing—in fact, Sardinia has almost a half of all Italy's sheep. Shepherds practice transhumance (see Chapter 7) and spend many months of the year in

Sardinia

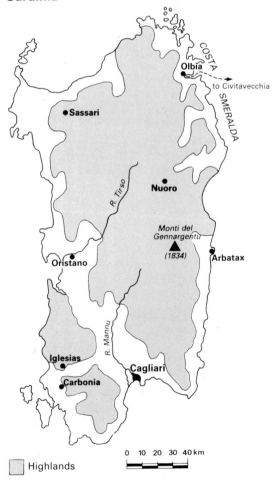

0 10 20 30 40 km

Highlands

the wilds with their animals. The men sleep in crude mountain shelters and eat almost nothing but bread, cheese and wine. This lonely life does not attract young people and most move away from the interior. Many shepherds have left Sardinia to find similar but easier work on mainland Italy.

Mining

Sardinia is not very industrialized although it has some of Italy's most important mineral supplies. In the south-west of the island there are two major mining towns. Carbonia is the main coal-producing centre of Italy (*carbone* is Italian for coal). It was developed by Mussolini in the 1930s but has been allowed to run down in the last few decades as oil takes the place of coal in the Italian economy. At Iglesias there are lead and zinc mines as well as a geological museum.

Cagliari

The capital and chief port of Sardinia is near coastal marshes and set in a broad gulf. Some parts of the marshes are used as salt-pans. The sea is allowed into shallow basins, the water evaporates in the summer heat and leaves behind crusts of salt. Cagliari is Italy's largest salt producer.

The port of Cagliari is not very big and most of the town is modern. In recent years large-scale industrial developments have given the town an economic boost.

The Costa Smeralda

The *Costa Smeralda* (or 'Emerald Coast') is Sardinia's biggest tourist development and has brought the island into keen competition with other Mediterranean holiday resorts. Situated in the north-east of the island where there are fine sandy beaches and attractive rocky head-lands, numerous luxury hotels and sports facilities have been built to bring in rich tourists. In recent years Sardinia has become the most popular summer holiday centre for Italians and has also attracted thousands of foreign visitors.

The Costa Smeralda

The centre of Cagliari

Questions

1 Why do you think Sardinia has kept its own distinctive character?
2 How does the interior of Sardinia differ from the interior of Sicily?
3 What do you think of the way of life of a Sardinian shepherd? What are the pleasant aspects of his way of life?
4 Why do you think coal has declined in relation to oil in the Italian economy?
5 What are lead and zinc used for?
6 What tells you that the Costa Smeralda development aims at the rich end of the tourist market?
7 Which is the main ferry port for Sardinia on the Italian mainland?

For further research

In what ways is the culture of Sardinia different from that of mainland Italy? What customs do the Sardinians follow? Does their life style resemble that of the Sicilians in any way?

41

Revision: Section One

I   Unjumble these words to form the names of Italian cities:

RIBA	SPLANE	COLENERF
CEIVEN	LAMIN	GANOBLO
ELOMPRA	INURT	SAIP

II   Find the odd one out:

1   Po, Tiber, Arno, Sila, Ticino
2   Maggiore, Bracciano, Comacchio, Como, Larderello
3   Etna, Vesuvius, Gran Sasso, Vulcano, Stromboli
4   Brindisi, Rome, Genoa, Livorno, Venice
5   Maremma, Elba, Sicily, Sardinia, Tremiti

III   What are the following?

trulli transhumance *cascine* centuriation tuffs *fumare*

IV   In which *regioni* would you expect to find?

1   The leaning tower of Pisa
2   St Peter's Basilica
3   Vesuvius
4   The main FIAT motorworks
5   *Città contadine*
6   The 'Certosa' of Pavia
7   The southern end of the Appian Way
8   A swordfish fishing fleet
9   More sheep than people.
10   Bears, wolves and wild goats in a National Park

V   True or false?

1   Emilia-Romagna is part of the *Mezzogiorno*.
2   The Arabs ruled over Calabria for two hundred years.
3   Aosta has an important steelworks.
4   The Italian stock-exchange is located in Rome.
5   San Marino is an independent kingdom.
6   Catania was destroyed by an earthquake in 1972.
7   Gargano is a peninsula in Apulia.
8   Tobacco may be seen growing in Umbria.
9   Italy's naval academy is in Genoa.
10   The Vatican has its own radio station, newspaper and railway.

VI   Multiple choice:

1   *Asti Spumante* wine comes from Tuscany/Lazio/Sicily/Piedmont.
2   There is a tuna cannery at Favignana/Parma/Cagliari/Bari.
3   Iglesias is famous for its cathedral/ski-slopes/lead and zinc mines/citrus fruits.
4   Ferries go to Greece from Civitavecchia/Brindisi/Livorno/Rimini.
5   Geothermal energy is generated in Lombardy/Campania/Apulia/Tuscany.
6   The highest mountain in Italy is M. Rosa/Corno Grande/Etna/M. Amiata.
7   Italy's second largest city is Milan/Turin/Naples/Genoa.
8   *Mozzarella* cheese is made from the milk of cows/sheep/goats/buffaloes.
9   The isle of Capri is made of volcanic ash/granite/limestone/soft clays.
10   The Pontine Marshes were drained during the 10th/15th/18th/20th century.

Section two: The Italian way of life

18 City Life

Italy has a longer tradition of city life than most other European countries. In Roman times they were highly organized and their inhabitants had all sorts of facilities, including piped water and sewage disposal. During the Middle Ages, when many central Italian cities set themselves up as independent states, people were proud of their cities. Today, the larger Italian cities have many characteristics common to cities the world over—skyscraper blocks, heavy industry and traffic jams—but their historic centres give them a strong identity of their own. Most smaller cities have an unmistakable centre made up of such buildings as the cathedral, town hall and ducal palace. They are grouped round a central *piazza*, or square, which is a favourite meeting place for local people.

The daily routine

Town life in Italy starts early—buses and trams are already working by 5.30 a.m., and many people are on their way to work by 7.00 a.m. Some have long, slow journeys ahead of them as they pass through rush-hour traffic. Bars are generally open from at least 6.30 and people gather in them for a cup of coffee on their way to work. Market stall-holders too are busy setting out their produce before 7 a.m. Shops open from 8.00 onwards and, especially in the hotter months, housewives are out buying their daily food soon afterwards.

Shops remain open until 1.00 p.m. and then close for several hours during the afternoon. Factories and some offices keep similar hours which means that Italian families generally eat together at lunchtime. (Children are home from school by about 1.45 p.m.) After lunch is the *siesta* when people rest or sleep until it is time to go back to work. The *siesta* is especially useful in the height of summer when the afternoon heat is almost too great for people to go out on the streets.

City streets get crowded with cars and people from 5 p.m. onwards as some people finish work and others do their evening shopping. One or two places, however, get extremely crowded during the *passeggiata*. Before they return home for the family supper, Italians love to walk up and down a particular stretch of main street or around a *piazza* with their friends, chatting and passing the time of day. This *passeggiata* is very popular with young people as it gives them a chance to show off their latest clothes and have a good look at one another.

As the shops pull down their shutters at either 7.30 or 8.00 p.m. (the time varies between winter and summer) the streets gradually empty for the rest of the night. Only certain areas of the towns, for example those with restaurants, cinemas and nightclubs, get crowded again after supper.

Modern blocks of flats in Rome

Questions

1 Why does Italy have such a strong city-dwelling tradition?
2 What features make Italian cities different from cities elsewhere?
3 Do you think it is a good thing to have a long lunch break and *siesta?*
4 Do you think that shop-keepers' lives are difficult with the long hours that they work?
5 Are Italian flats better adapted to winter or summer conditions?
6 What do kitchens tell us about the Italian way of life?

Crowds gathering at lunchtime in a town's main *piazzà*

Town housing

In the old centres of Italian cities many families live in blocks built in the Middle Ages. Their flats have thick stone walls which keep them relatively warm in winter and cool in summer. But the buildings are difficult to keep in good repair and are often without lifts and other facilities.

In the 16th to 19th centuries great palaces were built and divided into apartments for members of rich aristocratic families to live in. In modern Italy, all large blocks are referred to as *palazzi* (palaces), however new. Most of these are under private ownership as there is little council housing in Italy.

One of the most striking features inside Italian flats is the flooring, for which polished marble slabs or coloured glazed tiles are commonly used. These keep the rooms cool in summer but need to be covered with warm rugs during the winter. Most *palazzi* have central heating which is turned on for at least four months of the year.

Nearly all houses have shutters which can be let down in summer to keep the heat out. Balconies and terraces are an important part of Italian life as they provide a place to hang the washing, and frequently also somewhere to sit and chat to the next-door neighbour. Bigger terraces may be decorated with potted plants and grapevines. They make excellent places to eat outside in the scented air of a hot summer's night.

Living rooms are not very different from those elsewhere in Europe, with furniture either modern or in a more heavily carved traditional style. A television is generally placed in a prominent position. Kitchens are usually large and well equipped. Italians attach great importance to food and many hours will be spent every day preparing meals. All the correct utensils are very necessary!

Not all town-dwellers live in flats. In the rich and fashionable areas of Italian cities there are large villas, many of them dating from the last century, set behind trees in walled gardens. At the other extreme some southern cities, such as Palermo and Naples, have baracche or shanty towns. Here there are narrow unmade roads lined with single-storeyed houses made of brick and wood and often without running water. Poor families from the surrounding countryside settle in these shanty towns because they are unable to afford proper accommodation.

19 Life in the Country

Approximately one in ten Italians lives in the countryside and works on the land under conditions which have not changed greatly in hundreds of years. As visitors travel around Italy they are often struck by the large hill-top villages which were built either before or during the Middle Ages as a means of protecting their people against attack.

Most country-dwellers live in such villages but there are many different types of rural settlement in Italy. In parts of the Northern Plain, Tuscany and Apulia there are large estate farms which have several families living in them. These are more common than villages. By contrast in the *trulli* zone of Apulia and on the various reclaimed marshlands of the Italian peninsula, farmers live in modest houses built on their smallholdings.

Donkeys still used for village transport

The old pattern of life

The daily routine of many country people is still that of the traditional peasant farmer. This is especially true of the older people as few young people want to work such long hours. Crops and animals need a lot of attention and so the best has to be made of daylight hours. Farmers and their wives are on their way to the fields soon after sunrise, often on foot, by donkey or by horse and cart. They work there until nightfall, tilling the ground, tending the vines and olives, feeding and

45

Small-scale farming machinery can tackle difficult land

milking the animals and keeping walls and fences in good repair. A lot of hard manual work is involved, especially where the land is of poor quality. Much of the produce goes to feed the farmer and his family and the rest goes to market.

When the workers return home they eat supper and go to bed early, ready to get up again at sunrise the following day. Only on Sundays is this routine broken and the farmer and his family take a well-earned day of rest.

There were few entertainments in such villages before the coming of radio and television. Most women still remain at home and look after the children while the men go to drink wine and play cards at a local bar.

Housing in the country

In the country there are many regional variations in housing. In the Alps, the wooden steep-roofed chalet is common. It is sometimes two-storeyed with the family's living area above and a cattle byre with hay store below. By contrast the small, single-storeyed, whitewashed stone cottage is typical of many parts of Basilicata, Calabria and Sicily.

Country homes are generally much simpler inside than town houses. The most important item of furniture is a big wooden table which dominates the living room, and emphasises the importance of family meals in the daily routine. Old-fashioned stoves have the dual purpose of cooking (many country people make their own bread) and keeping the home warm in winter. Country dwellers are on the whole devoutly religious and the plain walls of their cottage interiors are often hung with a crucifix and pictures of the Virgin Mary and other saints.

46

The changing way of life

Since the end of the last century the remoter and poorer villages have had a constant stream of people leaving them to go to other parts of Italy and abroad in search of jobs. These have been mainly young people so villages are left with a population where the average age is much higher than that of the towns and cities. Two things are now beginning to reverse this trend; the modernization of housing and agriculture and the fact that many city dwellers have bought up abandoned cottages and made them into holiday and weekend homes.

More and more villages are now made up of two distinct areas: the old stone-built medieval section with narrow, cobbled and stepped streets unsuited to motor traffic, and a more planned, modern area. The blocks of flats in the modern areas are lower than those in the cities but otherwise very similar. Donkeys and horse-drawn carts are rapidly becoming a thing of the past as small motorbikes, three-wheeled trucks and mini-tractors are now just as cheap for farmers to buy.

Ten years ago many villagers had to go to communal pumps or wells for their daily water supply and relied on oil-lamps for their lighting. Now most villages have piped water and are connected to the main electricity supply.

Although life may still be much harder in villages than in towns, there are the outward signs of 20th-century living with the flicker of TV sets, the noise of teenagers on motorbikes and the attraction of electronic 'space invader' games in the bars.

Narrow cobbled village streets

Peasant woman with her handicrafts

Questions

1 Why was the traditional way of life of a peasant farmer and his wife so difficult?
2 How does their way of life differ from that of a city dweller?
3 Why do you think houses in the Alps are so different from those in southern Italy?
4 What are the main changes affecting village communities today?
5 Which of these changes are good for the villagers and which are bad?

For further research

Find out more about the way in which people live in rural areas of your country. How is it different from the Italian situation? Are there any similarities?

47

20 Italian Food

Different types of pasta

Italians take great delight in eating and have a wide variety of food to choose from. Traditional Italian cooking is different from one part of the country to another and many places give their names to regional dishes. Italian food can be enjoyed in many different parts of the world, however, because of the many Italians who have set up restaurants abroad.

Pasta

At the mention of Italian food most people think of *spaghetti*—which is just one of many types of *pasta*. *Pasta*, the Italian word for dough, is made from the flour of *grano duro* (hard wheat) together with water and olive oil. Sometimes eggs are added to make *pasta all'uovo*. Said to have been introduced into Italy from China by Marco Polo, *pasta* is made into all sorts of shapes and sizes and has a wide variety of names. *Fettucine, tagliatelle* and *linguine* (meaning little tongues) are all flat types of *pasta*, whereas *macaroni, rigatoni* and *penne* are tube-like (*penne* literally means 'pens' because they are cut at angles like the old quill pens). Some of the more fanciful pasta names include *fusile*, which are spiral and named after the bore of a rifle, and *paglia e fieno* (hay and straw) which is a mixture of yellow *pasta* made with eggs and green pasta made with spinach.

Pasta is served with a wide range of sauces. Some of the most popular are *bolognese* (a meat sauce which originated in Bologna), *al pesto* (made with chopped basil, garlic, cheese and oil), *all'arabbiata* (which means 'enraged' because of the use of hot chilli peppers) and *all'amatriciana* (with tomatoes and ham—named after a small town in the Central Apennines and *alla Carbonara* (see recipe).

Some of the best-known types of *pasta* are served stuffed with meat or soft *ricotta* cheese and spinach. *Ravioli* are cushion shaped and *cannelloni* are like rolled, stuffed pancakes.

Meat and fish

Although it sometimes follows *antipasto, pasta* is generally referred to as a *primo piatto* or 'first course', which is then followed by a main course of meat or fish.

Veal (*vitello*) is the most popular Italian meat and is served up in a wide variety of ways. A very simple veal dish is *cotoletta alla milanese*—veal cutlet deep fried in breadcrumbs. More adventurous are the Roman dishes such as *saltimbocca*, slices of veal with ham, cheese and sage, and *involtini*, veal rolls stuffed with vegetables.

Beef is normally grilled, as are pork and lamb. Pigs and sheep are often slaughtered young to produce *maialino* (sucking pig) and *agnello* (young lamb).

Chicken is a popular dish in Italy and is served in many different ways. Game birds, such as *fagiani* (pheasants) and *quaglie* (quail) are on many restaurant menus, as is *cinghiale* (wild boar) during the game season.

Recipe for 'Spaghetti alla Carbonara'

For six people

600 grammes spaghetti
200 grammes bacon, thinly sliced
1 clove of garlic, crushed
1 dessertspoon olive oil
5 eggs
1–2 tablespoons single cream (optional)
1 tablespoon finely chopped parsley
¼ teaspoon finely grated lemon peel
salt and lots of freshly ground black pepper
100 grammes grated parmesan cheese

Cook the spaghetti in lots of boiling, salted water. While it is cooking, lightly sauté the bacon with the oil, and when nearly done add the garlic, taking care not to let it brown. Keep hot while the pasta finishes cooking. Lightly beat the eggs in a bowl with the cream, salt and pepper, parsley and lemon peel. (The addition of the cream makes a slightly richer dish.)

When the pasta is '*al dente*' (i.e. cooked, but still slightly chewy) strain well and put back into the saucepan. Quickly add the bacon, with the oil it cooked in, and then add the eggs. Mix rapidly for a few moments and then serve, covered with lots of parmesan cheese.

Mediterranean fish

Questions

1 Why do so many Italian dishes have place names in them?
2 Do you think that Italians eat an interesting variety of food?
3 Why are there always some fresh fruits and vegetables available in Italy?
4 In which other countries of the world would you expect to find Italian restaurants? Why?

The Mediterranean produces a wide range of seafood. Swordfish are so large that they have to be sliced into 'steaks'. Tuna is generally tinned rather than eaten fresh. *Gamberi* (prawns), *calamari* (squid), *polpi* (octopus) and *scampi* are favourite ingredients of mixed seafood dishes and usually deep fried in batter or grilled and served with oil, lemon and parsley. Shellfish are another popular item in the Italian diet. *Vongole* (small clams) are generally made into a sauce for spaghetti, while *cozze* (mussels) are served as a dish on their own.

Fresh fruit and vegetables

The Mediterranean climate makes it possible to have some fresh vegetables and fruit all year round. There are always some salad ingredients available and either these or cooked greens are the most common type of side dish served with the main course. The more specifically Mediterranean vegetables such as *peperoni* (sweet peppers), *melanzane* (aubergines), *carciofi* (artichokes) and *zucchine* (baby marrows) have a more limited season.

As the different fruit harvests take place the market stall and *frutteria* stocks change. For example, citrus fruits are common in the spring, water melons at the height of the summer and grapes in the early autumn. Fresh fruits are generally on restaurant menus as *frutta di stagione* (fruit of the season) and are also made into *macedonia* (fruit salad).

Italian desserts

Italy is the home of ice-cream. Traditionally believed to be a Neapolitan invention, a sort of ice-cream was made in ancient Roman times from snow brought down from the Apennines. Modern *gelati* are delicious and served in an extraordinary range of fruit, nut and other flavours. In restaurants they may be served as *gelati affogati*, 'drowned' in liqueur.

Italy also produces a wide range of cakes and tarts which may be served to round off a meal. One of these, *montebianco*, combines meringue, whipped cream, flaky pastry and chestnut purée to produce a very sweet, but excellent, dessert.

Fresh artichokes in a market

49

Italy produces more wine than any other nation in the world. This is nothing new. The ancient Greeks called Italy *Enotria*—'the land of wine' because so much of the country was under grapevines. The climate throughout Italy is ideal for the ripening of grapes and it is only on land above 1000 metres that vines are not grown. The best places are hilly areas where both soil and drainage are good.

Vineyards

Over two million hectares of Italy are under grapevines, and much of this land has been carefully terraced out of steep hillsides. Grapevines are creepers. They are either trained to grow along wires stretched between wooden and concrete poles or allowed to entwine themselves in rows of regularly planted trees, such as maples, poplars and mulberries. This keeps the grapes off the ground.

About one-third of Italy's vineyards operate the system of *cultura promiscua* (known in English as 'interculture'). Vines are planted in fields along with other crops—including olives, peaches, citrus fruits and almonds.

Vines require a lot of attention. In spring they must be trained and in June they are sprayed with copper sulphate solution to kill pests. In the main growing season, between July and October, the grapes are carefully inspected and birds kept at bay.

A lot of Italy's grape production is still in the hands of small farmers, although the large estates dominate the market. In the past, owners of small-holdings would pick their own grapes and make them into wine in their own cellars. Nowadays these farmers tend to take their grapes to large cooperatives which produce bulk quantities of wine.

It is difficult to mechanize the picking of grapes so in October farmers hire many extra workers to complete the *vendemmia* (harvest). Grapes are picked in bunches with either a sharp knife or secateurs.

Wine making

The harvested grapes are first put into vats and crushed. The solids (skins, pips and stalks) are then removed and the liquid left to ferment for a few days. After this it is either put into barrels or bottled.

The strength of the wine depends upon its sugar content, which in turn depends upon the amount of heat the grapes got while they were ripening. The alcohol content is much higher in the wines produced in Southern Italy and Sicily than those from the North.

The wine-producing regions

Italy produces about 75 million hectolitres of wine a year. Although every *regione* has its vineyards the national production is concentrated in certain areas.

The northern wines are generally the best in quality and the two regions of Veneto and Piedmont are particularly important. Three of Veneto's most famous wines are the white *Soave*, the red *Valpolicella* and

Cultura promiscua

Harvesting the grapes

Stirring the grapes in a wooden vat

Questions

1 Look at the relief map in Chapter 1. What proportion of Italy is unsuitable for grapevine cultivation?
2 Why do you think grapes should be kept off the ground while growing?
3 Why do vines need a lot of attention?
4 Why do you find Italian wines with the highest alcohol content in western Sicily?
5 Name two volcanic areas of Italy which are important for wine.

the light red *Bardolino*. Piedmont has its production concentrated around the Asti area (see Chapter 4).

Industrial Lombardy has quite a lot of land under vines but its best wines come from the large Alpine trough, Valtellina. Tuscany has many famous wine centres in its hill country, including Siena, San Gimignano, Montepulciano and Montalcino, and produces fine red and white wines. Lazio's vineyards are concentrated in the volcanic hill country to the north and south of Rome (see Chapter 12). One of Lazio's best wines has the strange name *Est! Est!! Est!!!* The story goes that in 12th century a German bishop was journeying to Rome and sent a man ahead to taste the wines for him. The bishop told him to write the Latin word *est* ('it is') on the door of every tavern selling good wine. The man was so impressed by the wine he found at Monte-fiascone on the slopes of Lake Bolsena that he wrote *Est! Est!! Est!!!* on the tavern door.

In Campania vine growing is concentrated around the Bay of Naples. Its most famous wines are those produced on the slopes of Mount Vesuvius and called *Lacryma Christi*—'the tears of Christ'. Apulia is Italy's biggest producer of strong wines. Much of its output is sent north to mix with wines which are low in alcohol content.

Western Sicily is the home of *Marsala*. This is a very strong amber-coloured wine which was 'discovered' by two Englishmen in the 18th century, John Woodhouse and Benjamin Ingram. Each of them set up a large profitable business in the town of Marsala. The wine of the area was already strong because of the high summer temperatures but they also fortified it (by adding alcohol), and produced a wine similar to sherry. Today the various *Marsala* firms are in the hands of Sicilians and the wine is one of the island's main exports.

The labels of some famous Italian wines

Restaurants

Eating out is an important part of the Italian way of life. Italian restaurants are lively places where people go to talk as well as to enjoy their food and drink. During the summer months the tables spill out onto the busy pavements.

There are many names for eating places in Italy. A *ristorante* is an expensive town restaurant where you would expect to be served by waiters wearing bow ties. A *trattoria* is more reasonably priced and often specializes in regional dishes. An *osteria*, originally just a drinking place, provides only simple food. Nowadays, the distinctions between them are not so great.

Meals in Italy have four or five courses and may last for two or three hours. And restaurants are not just for adults. It is quite usual to see small children eating dinner with the rest of the family until eleven o'clock at night. However, Sunday lunchtime is the favourite time for the whole family to eat together in a restaurant.

Pizza is a familiar dish all over the world and in Italy *pizzerie* are popular eating places, especially with young people. They are a cheap, fast alternative to the traditional restaurant.

Self-service restaurants have not really caught on in Italy as people still like to take time over their meals. The *tavola calda* (literally 'hot table') is the nearest equivalent. In these the customer chooses from various cooked dishes which are on display at the counter.

Waiters serving at a *ristorante*

At a pavement cafe

Bars

Even the smallest of Italian towns may have a dozen bars. As well as being social meeting places bars are where most people go to make telephone calls. (Telephone kiosks are rare in Italy.)

Characteristic features of an Italian bar are the stainless steel counter, the hissing of the *espresso* machine, the rattling of coffee cups and rows of bottles of different drinks on the shelves behind the counter. The hard-working barman continuously cleans the counter and always re-washes glasses and cups just before using them.

Most of the year there are a few tables outside in the street, for even in winter it is pleasant to sit outside at midday. There are two price lists, one for having a drink at the bar and the other, with an added service charge, for sitting at the tables.

Many Italians eat breakfast in a bar. This is often just a coffee with a horn-shaped pastry called a *cornetto*. There are three main ways of drinking coffee: black or *espresso*; white, known as a *capuccino* after the colour of a Franciscan monk's habit; and the very milky, *caffe latte*.

Some bars, especially in the south, offer no food other than *cornetti*. Others have sandwiches (*tramezzini*) and ham or cheese-filled rolls (*panini*).

Bars are open all day. They are most crowded just before mealtimes, when people drop in to drink an *aperitivo*, such as vermouth, and just after a meal when people drink a *digestivo* like brandy or *grappa*, and coffee.

Some bars specialize in ice-cream and are known as *gelaterie*. These are very popular with children, especially during the summer months, and are frequently visited for the final course after a large meal.

A more old-fashioned type of drinking place is the *cantina* or wine cellar. This is still mainly a male preserve. It is most common in the important wine-producing villages, but can still be found in some of the larger cities. Typically, these cool, dark rooms are lined with barrels and old men sit wearing their trilby hats telling stories, playing cards and drinking wine.

Questions

1 In which type of Italian restaurant would you expect to buy the cheapest meal?
2 Why do major meals in Italy last two or three hours?
3 Why do you think self-service restaurants are so popular outside Italy, yet not in Italy itself?
4 How do Italian bars differ from pubs?
5 On average, how many times would an Italian visit a bar during the day and for what purposes?
6. How does a *cantina* differ from an ordinary Italian bar?

23 Money, Shops and Markets

Questions

1 Do you know of any other country where inflation has caused such large denomination notes to be printed?
2 Why do you think Italian markets are so crowded?
3 Do you think it sounds fun to buy food in Italy?
4 Why do you think supermarkets are not so popular in Italy?
5 How do the old craft and repair-shops compare to similar places in your country?

Italian money

The Italian unit of currency is the lira. Dramatic inflation has taken place throughout the 20th century so the single lira no longer exists. The smallest denomination coin, worth almost nothing, is 10 lire. Of highest value is the 100,000 lire note. When buying things like houses and cars Italians have to think in terms of millions of lire!

Markets

Italian housewives like to buy their food fresh and going to market is an important part of their daily routine. All towns and even small villages have daily fruit and vegetable markets. They generally have meat and cheese stalls too. The markets are crowded and often it is quite a struggle to fight through them. In places close to the sea there are also fish markets.

A vegetable market in Rome

Shops

There is a wide variety of the small, traditional type of shop in Italy. Many still have pull-down shutters which fill the streets with a characteristic rattling sound at opening and closing times. These are similar to the shops of two thousand years ago which can still be seen in archaeological sites such as Pompeii and Trajan's Market in Rome.

There are many different sorts of food shop. The general grocer's is most commonly called an *alimentari* and is frequently a family concern. The *frutteria* is the greengrocer's and often has a magnificent display of fruit and vegetables arranged just outside the doorway to entice passers-by. Shopkeepers in Italy take great pride in the way they arrange their wares. They see it as the best possible form of advertisement to the general public. The *macelleria* is the butcher's shop. The meat is cut on huge slabs of marble, which are rigorously scrubbed clean every evening.

Supermarkets have not caught on as widely in Italy as they have elsewhere in Europe and the USA. Italians still like personal service when buying food. The number of supermarkets is growing, however, and even hypermarkets have been built on the outskirts of the largest cities.

When buying clothes many people still go to the tailor's shop or *sartoria*, but younger Italians are attracted to the smaller 'boutiques' where the latest fashions are available.

Many traditional craftsmen have workshops in the older quarters of Italian cities and they still charge reasonable prices for their goods. There are also specialist repair-shops where you can get almost anything mended, whether it is a complicated piece of machinery or just a shoe.

The larger stores

Italy, like most countries, has its 'chain stores'. The two main ones 'Standa' and 'Upim' can be found in every town. A wide range of goods is on sale in these stores including toys, stationery, clothing and kitchen ware. There is often a food section too.

Department stores are not as common. In the biggest cities there may be one or two, but Italian shopping centres do not have row upon row of great towering buildings. They are more like the high street of a small market town.

Tourist shopping

Most parts of Italy are on the tourist routes so many shops specialize in goods for sale to foreign visitors. In Venice the coloured glass of the island of Murano is of high quality. In the hill towns of Tuscany and Umbria there is a long history of making pottery and shops have fine patterned ceramics on display. The most popular tourist souvenirs from Sicily are the traditional knight-in-armour puppets.

This picture shows a pork butcher's shop. Its name *norcineria* is after the Umbrian town of Norcia famous for its pig products.

Inside a department store

55

24 Fashion and Dress

Italians are very fashion-conscious. It is important to them to be wearing the right thing at the right time, to look neat and tidy and to create a good impression. They are a well-dressed nation and look good in what they wear on both formal or informal occasions.

The fashion trade

Milan, like Paris and New York, is one of the great centres of the fashion business. Top Italian designers show a number of collections there each year and fashion trade people come from all over the world to see them. Milan often sets the fashion trends which other countries then follow.

Milan developed this special role as a result of being the centre of the great textile-producing area of Lombardy. For centuries this area produced fine woollens and silks which it exported all over Europe. Several Milanese fashion houses still get most of their materials from Lombardy.

Throughout Italy there are thousands of boutiques and clothes shops offering the latest fashions. Young people in particular spend a large proportion of their income on what they wear. Clothes shops, like other shops in Italy, have very attractive window-displays which are extremely luring to the young. In the streets people take great interest in what others are wearing and enjoy passing comments on it.

Fashion shops in the centre of Rome

Regional costumes

Old photographs of Italian villages at the turn of the century show both men and women wearing traditional regional peasant costumes. Each region of Italy—and in some places each village—had a distinctive outfit which people wore either every day or just on Sundays and other holidays. Traditional costume now survives in only a few isolated places and it is generally only the older women who wear it. At Scanno, a small mountain village in the Abruzzi, many of the women wear the traditional long black pleated skirt and blouse. In Pisticci, a whitewashed hill town of Basilicata, the older women still dress in their long dark skirts and white baggy blouses with bodices. But these are two rare examples. In most villages the tradition has died out but, when widowed, women still wear black for the rest of their lives.

People in uniform

Visitors to Italy are often surprised by the large number of people wearing different types of uniform. For a start, Italy still has national service and there are young soldiers of various regiments wearing their uniforms around the streets of most main cities. Then there are several different types of police force. The most important of these are the semi-military *Carabinieri* who wear black uniforms with a red stripe down their trousers. On ceremonial occasions *Carabinieri* guards may also be seen in cocked hats with a red and blue plume and carrying swords. The *vigili urbani* are the main traffic police and they wear a characteristic white helmet. Even bus drivers and railway personnel take great pride in their appearance and have smart official uniforms.

Perhaps the most colourful uniforms to be found in Italy are those designed over four hundred years ago by Michelangelo for the Papal Swiss Guard. These yellow and blue outfits are worn by soldiers from the Swiss army who come to the Vatican City in Rome to guard the Pope's palace.

Questions

1 Why did Milan develop into such an important fashion centre?
2 Why do you think that there has been a decline in regional costumes? Has this happened in your country?
3 What tells you that Italians take great pride in their appearance?
4 Do you know the names of any Italian fashion designers?
5 Why are there so many different types of uniform in Italy?

Swiss guards in their traditional uniform

Carabinieri **at work**

25 Family Life

Questions

1 What tells you that in many Italian families the boys are more favoured than the girls? Is this fair?
2 What are the advantages of people living in large family groups?
3 How many times would you expect a large family to gather together and celebrate during the course of the year?
4 What are the main problems caused by strong family ties and the emphasis upon family honour?
5 What do you understand by *mammismo?* Who do you think see it as a problem, men or women?

Italian families are large and close-knit. Although the average family size is much smaller than it was a few decades ago, it is still common, especially in the south, for couples to have eight or ten children. Grandparents and unmarried uncles or aunts may also live with a married couple with children, so Italian homes are often lively, crowded and noisy places. Large families have their advantages and disadvantages. Although there are more hands to share the housework (at least between the women), young people don't get much privacy with so many relations around.

Even when a small family unit lives on its own there are frequent family gatherings when brothers, sisters, aunts, uncles and cousins all get together to celebrate family occasions, such as christenings and weddings.

Two family events which are more common in Italy and other Roman Catholic countries than in northern Europe are first communions and *onomastici* or 'name-days'. Children generally go to church for their first communion when they are about nine. Girls dress in white, rather like brides, and boys have white habits like those worn by monks. After church, the large family group has a huge celebratory Sunday lunch which may last until five or six in the evening. The children are guests of honour. The *onomastico* takes place on the day of the saint after which someone is named. It is regarded by most Italians as being more important than a birthday. On a name-day the person celebrating is expected to treat his or her relations to a big meal.

Family ties

Italian families are very close and everyone gives support in times of trouble. This is sometimes taken to extremes during a dispute between families, and a *vendetta* develops. These *vendette* can give rise to tit-for-tat shootings between two families. They were much more common in the past but still occasionally break out and make national headlines.

Although the father is almost always the breadwinner of the family, the role of the mother is very strong and she is the one who provides stability. Some would argue that her presence is overbearing and that *mammismo*, as it is known, is a problem in Italy. Male children are often spoilt by their mothers and are frequently dominated by them for the rest of their lives.

Moral attitudes within the family

With such strong family ties and the great importance attached to family honour, divorce rates are low in Italy, especially in the South. People generally live at home until they get married and this gives the family plenty of time to scrutinize future in-laws. Also, financial circumstances often force newly-weds to live with their parents for a while until they can afford to set up their own homes.

Even if marriages are unsuccessful, the disgrace brought to a family by having a divorce within it often prevents that marriage from breaking up. Such family pressures have helped to make extra-marital affairs and prostitution common in Italy.

Brothers and sisters of a large family in Apulia.

26 Schools

In Italy education is compulsory between the ages of six and fourteen. Most children go to state schools but there are a few private and boarding schools. Many children under six are now going to nursery schools and more and more pupils over fourteen are now going on to specialist schools and then on to university.

Elementary schools

There are two types of school during the eight years of compulsory education. From the ages of six to eleven there are the *Scuole Elementare* (elementary schools) where children learn basic subjects like Italian, mathematics, history, geography, science and religious knowledge. It is rare that they do any sport, music or handicrafts. Pupils work six mornings a week, from 8.30 a.m. to 1.30 p.m., Mondays to Saturdays.

Middle schools

At eleven years of age, children go on to a *Scuola Media* (middle school) where they stay for three years. The range of subjects they are taught here is much wider than at elementary school. There is more science, many children have art and physical education lessons for the first time, and they also start courses in foreign languages. French and English are the most popular of these. Many aspects of Italian schools are still rather traditional and old-fashioned and pupil strikes and sit-ins aimed at changing the system are not unusual.

Scuola Media pupils also work a six-day week: either mornings or afternoons.

School holidays are affected by the Italian climate. Summer holidays are very long: from the end of June until the first days of October. Italian students, however, only have a few days off around Christmas and Easter, and half-term holidays do not exist.

Examinations are not just written. There is a written part to each exam but pupils are also questioned orally on each of their main subjects. The final year's examination, the *Terza Media*, is the most important. It is a school-leaving examination which is essential for going on to higher education and necessary for getting many types of job.

High schools

At fourteen, depending upon their performance in the *Scuola Media*, children can go on to one of many different types of school for the next five years. The most highly regarded of these high schools are the *Liceo Classico* and *Liceo Scientifico*. The *Liceo Classico* gives a good academic education specializing in the arts subjects—Italian, literature, history, political science and languages (including Latin and Greek). The *Liceo Scientifico* concentrates on the sciences.

In addition to the *Licei* there are several types of vocational school. In these pupils learn skills which will help them get on in a chosen career. These schools include the *Istituto Tecnico* (technical college) *Liceo Artistico* (art school) and *Liceo Linguistico* (language school). Their students are often involved in apprenticeships outside the schools as well as attending formal classes.

Elementary school pupils in their smocks

Questions

1 What are the advantages of going to school mornings only?

2 How many hours of schooling do Italian pupils do each week? How does that compare to your working week?

3 Do you think the Italian way of examining schoolchildren is better or worse than in your country?

4 Do you think the Italians get a good choice of high-school education? What are the advantages of this?

5 What are the main differences between the systems of education in Italy and in your country?

27 Politics

At the present time there are nine different political parties with seats in the national parliament and many in local government. This makes the governing of Italy both difficult and complicated—and most Italians have strong political opinions.

The political parties

Although it has rarely had a clear majority in parliament, the *Democrazia Cristiana* (Christian Democrat Party) has been in power continuously since 1947. The *DC* has close links with the Church. It is the successor of the old 'Popular Party' which was formed in the early 20th century by a priest in southern Italy.

The second largest party in Italy is the *Partito Comunista Italiano*, the *PCI*. This is the biggest Communist party in Europe outside the Communist bloc. The party at first followed the Russian model and was committed to overthrowing the government of Italy by revolutionary means. Today things are very different. Russia's invasion of Czechoslovakia in 1968 led the *PCI* to adopt a much more moderate style of communism, known as 'Eurocommunism'. Nevertheless the *PCI* encourages the strong anti-American feeling which is quite widespread in Italy. Although they have never been in control of national government, the *PCI* has ruled towns such as Florence and Bologna for many years.

Between these two large parties lies the *Partito Socialista Italiano (PSI)*, the third most popular group. Successive *DC* governments have relied upon *PSI* support. This has given the socialists quite a lot of say in the government of Italy.

Three smaller centre parties known collectively as the *Partiti Laici* are also important in the government of Italy. The *Partito Sociale Democratico Italiano* (Social Democrat Party) is a socialist faction which has broken away from the *PSI*. The *Partito Liberale Italiano* (Liberal Party) goes back to the ideas of the *Risorgimento* (see Chapter 45). The Republican Party, *Partito Repubblicano Italiano* also goes back to the nineteenth century for its inspiration and is regarded as the party with ideas of Mazzini. Although the *PRI* have only small electoral support, they gained the distinction of providing the first non-*DC* prime minister since the war, Giovanni Spadolini (in 1981).

The political extremes

On the far right of the political spectrum is the *Movimento Sociale Italiano*, the neo-Fascists. It is highly nationalistic and looks back to the strong-handed government of Mussolini's day. On the extreme left is the *Democrazia Proleteria (DP)*. This is one of several revolutionary socialist groups, but the only one represented in parliament. The small *Partito Radicale* (Radical Party) is relatively new but had sufficient impact on the general public to win seats in parliament when it first fought a general election (in 1976). The *PR* is fiercely anti-Vatican and actively supports such things as Women's Lib and the pro-abortion movement.

Banners at a Christian Democrat rally

Neo-Fascist graffiti

The electoral system

Everyone over the age of eighteen has the right to vote in a general election for the members of the *Camera dei Deputati* (the lower house of parliament). Italians have strong political opinions and elections always have a very high turnout. Special trains are put on to take workers back to their original homes where they have the vote. The constituencies vary in size but people can vote for more than one candidate.

A political cartoon

Pressure groups

A lot of political action in Italy takes place outside parliament. Some of the more extreme groups feel that they must resort to violent means of protest and occasionally this breaks out in the form of street riots. This type of political protest is now much less frequent than it was in the late 1960s and 1970s.

As in other European countries the trade unions have a lot of political influence and are brought in to discuss economic matters at high government level. There are many small unions but three big ones are dominant. They are *CISL* (*Confederazione Italiana Sindacati Lavoratori*) which is linked to the Christian Democrats; *CGIL* (*Confederazione Generale Italiana del Lavoro*) which is the Communist union; and *UIL* (*Unione Italiano del Lavoro*) which is Socialist.

In a society which is so dominated by the family and the traditions of the Roman Catholic Church many of the social reform movements which have been successful in Northern Europe have been slow to catch on in Italy. Only now are groups such as Women's Lib (*Movimento delle Donne*) beginning to make a political impact.

Questions

1 What do you think has helped the *DC* party remain in power for so long?
2 Why do you think some Italians would be worried about the *PCI* coming to power?
3 Does the Church have any political influence in your country? Do you think it is a good thing for the Roman Catholic Church to have political influence in Italy?
4 What is a 'pressure group'?
5 Why should the strength of the family make social reform difficult in Italy?

61

28 The Church

White smoke coming from the Sistine Chapel when John-Paul II was elected

Pope John-Paul II at a Wednesday general audience

The Church has a strong influence upon the Italian way of life and every town is dominated by the towers or domes of its main churches. For centuries the Pope was a major political figure in Italy. He ruled like a king over the central part of the country until 1870.

The Roman Catholic Church

The Holy Land was a part of the Roman Empire when Christ was crucified in Jerusalem. Some of his followers came to Rome to preach the new Christian faith. In about AD 67, St Peter was put to death by the Emperor Nero and was buried near the Vatican Hill. In the early 4th century, when Christianity was legalized, a huge basilica was built over the site of his burial. St Peter's successors, the Bishops of Rome, emerged as the most powerful religious figures in Europe. As 'father' of the Church, the Bishop of Rome took the title *Papa*, from which the English word Pope is derived.

Today there are 700 million Roman Catholics in the world. Many make a pilgrimage to Rome, and the Basilica and Square of St Peter have large crowds of visitors throughout the year. The Pope appears to pilgrims twice a week: once for his 'general audience' when he preaches a sermon, and once on Sundays at midday when he blesses the crowds.

Papal elections

Popes are elected by what is known as the 'College of Cardinals'. When a Pope dies, the cardinals are summoned from all over the world to the Vatican. Here they meet in secret *conclave* until they elect a successor. (The word *conclave* means 'with key'.) There are generally one or two ballots a day until one particular cardinal secures enough votes. Each time a ballot takes place the papers are burned in a special stove in the Sistine Chapel. The chimney of the stove is the only link between the cardinals and the outside world. If the ballot is unsuccessful the voting papers are burnt with chemicals to give off black smoke. When someone is elected the smoke is white.

Following his election, the new pope appears on the balcony of St Peter's to speak to a huge crowd in the Square below. Recently there were two conclaves in the same year. In 1978 John-Paul I was elected but he died a month later. The second conclave elected the Polish John-Paul II, the first non-Italian pope for 550 years.

Italians and the Church

Nearly all Italians are christened Roman Catholics but the extent to which people's behaviour and attitudes are influenced by Catholicism varies a lot. The older Italians tend to follow the Church's moral teaching more strictly than the young.

Until very recently the Church had sufficient power to prevent liberal laws on such issues as divorce and abortion going through Parliament. This is no longer so and many Italians resent what they see as the Church interfering in politics.

Religious shrines

There are many churches in Rome built on the tombs of early Christian martyrs. Underneath the city are the *catacombs*—a vast network of underground burial chambers scooped out of the soft volcanic rocks. Throughout Italy there are important places of pilgrimage associated with various saints or religious events. The most frequently visited of these include the Basilica of St Francis in Assisi, the Abbey of Monte Cassino founded by St Benedict, and St Mark's Basilica in Venice.

Italian churches

Italian churches vary considerably in style, but their interiors tend to be elaborately decorated. Walls are covered with colourful paintings of the lives of the saints and there is a great deal of gold leaf ornament on crosses and candlesticks. Probably the most distinctive features of Italian churches are the statues of the Virgin Mary and other saints. Made of wood or plaster and highly painted, they stand in ornate recesses with many rows of candles at their feet.

Questions

1 Why was St Peter in Rome during Nero's persecutions?
2 Why is the Pope an easy victim for an assassination attempt?
3 Do you think that the method of electing the Pope is old-fashioned?
4 What are the advantages of the cardinals meeting in *conclave*?
5 Do you think that the Roman Catholic Church had too much influence over the Italian people in the past?
6 Why is Italy such an important place for pilgrimage?
7 How are the interiors of Italian churches different from those in your country?

The interior of an Italian village church

63

29 Festivals

This picture shows the statue of San Domenico covered in live snakes being carried through the streets of Cocullo. It is believed that this ceremony stops children from being attacked by venomous snakes in this rocky, mountainous locality.

Questions

1 Why did the Italian government reduce the number of public holidays?
2 Why is Easter an important time for festivals? Is it the same in your country?
3 Do you think the food and drink festivals started in Christian or pre-Christian times? Why?
4 How are festivals good for the Italian economy?

Italy is a country which loves festivals. Until recently there were a dozen or so major public holidays, or *feste*, which commemorated various important events in the Christian calendar. The government has reduced these, however, to cut the amount of work-time lost and to bring Italy more into line with her EEC partners. The Roman Catholic Church cooperated by moving some of the festivals to the nearest Sunday.

A religious procession in Rome

Religious festivals

The most important religious festivals in Italy are those connected with Easter. *Settimana Santa*—the 'Holy Week' leading up to Easter—is a time for processions through the streets of many Italian cities. At Taranto in Apulia men belonging to various 'fraternities', wearing long hoods with eye-slits, carry statues, crosses and banners through the town's narrow streets on Good Friday. At Trapani in Sicily, a similar parade takes place on the evenings of Maundy Thursday and Good Friday when a series of huge and heavy wood carvings showing the scenes from Christ's passion are carried high on the shoulders of groups of men.

The patronal festival—on the saint's day of a particular village or church—is a day of great celebration for all concerned. Starting in the morning with a church service followed by a procession carrying the saint's statue through the streets, the celebrations go on all day. Brass bands, fairgrounds, stalls and an evening firework display often accompany the day's festivities.

Sometimes the ceremony of a local saint is mixed with a pagan rite which goes back way before Christianity came to Italy. One such example is at Cocullo in the Abruzzi (see photo).

Carnevale

Carnevale literally means 'goodbye to flesh'. During Lent—the six weeks leading up to Easter—Christians traditionally give up many of the pleasures of life. *Carnevale* is the last, wild celebration before Lent begins.

The common way of celebrating *Carnevale* was with mask or fancy dress parties and many still take place, especially in Venice. A more striking feature of *Carnevale* nowadays is the way in which children dress up in fanciful costumes—everything from princesses to 'Superman'—and at weekends parade around the main *passeggiata* streets throwing *confetti* at each other. In the past mothers made the children's costumes from any old materials they had available but today *Carnevale* has become a major commercial enterprise. Toyshops display expensive and elaborate costumes for months in advance. Some of the older children spend much of the *Carnevale* period running around the streets in gangs throwing eggs and flour, and squirting shaving foam at each other!

Children in *Carnevale* costume

Pageants and spectacles

Many festivals in Italy are not religious at all but go back to medieval times when towns enjoyed independent status. Venice is a fine example of this and has several historical *regate* (regattas) during the course of the year. The Grand Canal is covered with ornately painted barges and gondolas moving in formation or racing against each other. The most important of the Venetian festivals is the 'Wedding to the Sea'. This re-enacts the traditional ceremony where the Doge (the elected leader) went out into the lagoon and threw a golden ring into the water. This reminded people that the relationship between Venice and the sea was so close it was like a marriage.

Historical festivals where people dress up in medieval costume are common in Tuscany and Umbria. In Siena, Tuscany, the *Palio* is held twice every summer (see photo). This is a spectacular display of horse racing with the various *contrade*, or districts of the city, competing against each other. At Gubbio in Umbria in May in the *Corsa dei Ceri* (candle race) where three huge, ornately carved wooden candlesticks are raced through the streets on the shoulders of men dressed in the colours of the city's main quarters.

The *Palio* in Siena

Food and drink festivals

Harvest time has always been accompanied by festivities which celebrate the safe gathering in of the crops. The grape harvest is especially important in Italy and many places which produce wine have their *vendemmia* festivals. At Marino in the Colle Albani near Rome a fountain runs with wine for all to drink.

The food festivals which are held throughout Italy include all sorts of produce—cheese, mushrooms, strawberries and even artichokes have their *feste*. One important gastronomic event is the truffle festival held in such mountain towns as Norcia in Umbria. The very expensive and delicious truffles are collected from the woods to be sold in the markets and eaten in the restaurants.

For further research

In recent years there has been an ever increasing number of arts festivals in Italy. What is an arts festival? Find out about one of the following: the Venice Film Festival; the summer season of opera at Verona; the music and art festival at Spoleto.

65

30 Sport and Leisure

Questions

1 Why do you think sport is so popular in Italy?
2 What are the similarities and differences between football in Italy and in Britain?
3 What are the advantages and disadvantages of Sunday football?
4 Why do you think *bocce* is played in Italy rather than bowls?
5 Why is Italy so well-suited to skiing and swimming?

For further research

Find out about famous Italian sportsmen and women of the past and present.

A large proportion of Italians actively participate in sports and almost everyone follows the progress of a team or individual. Italy's climate allows people to spend a lot of their leisure time out of doors and many Italians take advantage of both the mountains and the sea. They spend at least one week in winter on the ski slopes and about a month in the summer soaking up the sunshine at a coastal holiday resort.

Popular sports

Football is without doubt the most popular sport in Italy. The game is called *calcio* (the Italian word for 'kick'). It was once known by its English name, but this was changed by Mussolini during one of his anti-English campaigns. Football is played widely at all levels from children kicking around in the street to Italy's top international team. The game is big business and the most important clubs such as *Juventus* of Turin, *Inter* of Milan and the Rome team, *Roma* buy and sell players for vast sums of money. Paolo Rossi, Italy's most famous football player, is not only a millionaire but one of the most popular subjects of the gossip magazines.

Sunday is the big day for football and thousands of noisy spectators cram into stadiums throughout Italy. A common sight on Sunday afternoons is men out with their wives having a *passeggiata*, holding a transistor radio firmly to their ear. Each week there are the football pools *totocalcio* on which millions of Italians gamble.

The Italian 1982 World Cup winning football team

Two racing sports are extremely popular in Italy: cycling and motor racing. Cycling is a sport for both the amateur and professional and at weekends hundreds of people are out training on the roads. Italy generally does well in international races such as the *Tour de France* and *Giro d'Italia*.

Italy is famous for its racing cars, such as Ferrari and Maserati, and has produced many world class racing drivers. It has a *Grand Prix* circuit at Monza, near Milan.

Interest in sport has increased as facilities throughout the country have improved. Young people are particularly keen on tennis and basketball which are two of the most popular games played at sports clubs. Every small town and village has its *campo sportivo* (sports ground) and there are fine modern sports centres in all the big cities.

Traditional games

In the villages and towns older men meet to play various traditional games. Most towns have a hard pitch for *bocce* either in a park or just by the roadside. *Bocce* is a game similar to bowls—small balls are thrown along the pitch to hit larger ones.

One of the oldest games in Italy is *mora* which was popular in ancient Rome and can be played in bars, on the streets or anywhere. It is simply a very quick guessing game where one person guesses the number of fingers held up simultaneously by another. People sitting in bars also enjoy card games and Italy has a traditional pack of playing cards which have batons, cups, discs and swords rather than hearts, clubs, diamonds and spades.

Leisure time

The time devoted to leisure is increasing throughout Europe and tourism within Italy is becoming more important each year. Motoring has long been a popular activity and at weekends roads are crowded. Shooting and fishing are two popular leisure pursuits among Italians who spend a lot of money getting the right sort of equipment and outfits.

Above all, the modern trend is towards buying holiday homes near the sea or in the mountains. Skiing and mountaineering as well as swimming, sailing and sub-aqua diving get a greater following each year and the holiday resort trade and property market are 'boom' industries.

Men playing *bocce*

Port Ercole, a fashionable yachting harbour in Tuscany

67

31   The Arts: Opera

Opera is the Italian word for 'work' and was the name given to a new type of musical stage work which developed in Italy during the 17th century. More operas have been written in Italian than in any other language and Italians still fill their numerous opera houses.

The evolution of opera

Opera has its origins back in the Renaissance. This revival of artistic interest during the 15th and 16th centuries included the writing of lots of new plays, many of which had incidental music composed specially for them. The scientific inventions of the period led to all kinds of mechanical devices being used to make stage productions more fantastic. During the 17th century leading characters often sang their parts rather than speak them, and *opera* was born.

Claudio Monteverdi is generally considered to be the first real opera composer. He was court musician to the Duke of Mantua between 1602 and 1612 and it was during this period that his first opera *Orfeo* was performed.

Questions

1 Do you think the Italian language is suited to opera?
2 What changes to drama, made during the Renaissance, eventually caused the evolution of opera?
3 Why do you think historical characters produce good themes for operatic entertainment?
4 Why did Mozart write some of his operas in Italian?
5 Why do sad love stories make good themes for operas?

For further research

Try and listen to some operatic music by Rossini and Puccini. Notice the difference between Italian opera at the beginning of this century and at the beginning of the last century.

or

Read the story of William Tell and then read about the political situation of Italy at the time of Rossini (See Chapter 45). What message do you think Rossini was trying to get across to the Italian people?

La Scala Opera House, Milan

Famous composers of Italian opera

Throughout the 18th century opera continued to develop. Common characteristics emerged such as plots which followed ancient legends or the lives of famous historical people. Special roles were written with individual singers in mind and there was always the need for sumptuous costumes and sets. One particular type of opera popular in 18th-century Italy was *opera buffa*. This was a comedy, often with a ridiculous plot, which delighted princes and citizens alike.

Famous composers at work in the early 18th century include Pergolesi and Piccini, both of whom spent much of their time in Naples, but their operas are rarely heard today. The best-known 18th-century Italian operas are in fact those of Mozart, written at the end of the century. He was Austrian but wrote operas based on Italian *libretti* as Italian had become the conventional language for this type of music. *Le Nozze di Figaro* (the Marriage of Figaro), *Don Giovanni* and *Così fan Tutte* are three of Mozart's greatest works.

The majority of Italian operas still popular today date from the 19th century when the composers Rossini, Donizetti, Bellini and Verdi were at work.

Rossini is best remembered for his comic operas such as 'The Barber of Seville', but some of his serious operas are also important. 'William Tell', the overture of which is still well-known, contained stirring patriotic ballads aimed at rousing Italian nationalism.

Donizetti and Bellini wrote a host of operas based upon characters from history and fiction. Important for them were the drama and passion of human situations, and generally their operas involved hero or heroine (or both) dying during the final climax. These two composers used such characters as Anne Boleyn, Lucrezia Borgia (daughter of Pope Alexander VI) and Romeo and Juliet as inspiration. Both were masters of what is known as *bel canto* (literally beautiful singing), giving their heroines complicated and beautiful arias which involved great 'vocal acrobatics'.

The greatest genius of 19th-century Italian opera was undoubtedly Giuseppe Verdi (who is dealt with more fully in Chapter 56).

Since Verdi, Puccini has been the only really outstanding Italian operatic composer. He worked from the late 19th century until the 1920s. Puccini's works, the most famous of which are *La Bohème*, *Tosca* and *Madame Butterfly*, are frequently performed today because of their rich soaring melodies and strong sad love stories.

Famous singers

It is not surprising that Italy has produced many great singers. During the 20th century many well-known Italian singers have become household names throughout the world. Probably most famous have been a succession of Italian tenors including Enrico Caruso (who recorded popular Neapolitan songs as well as opera) at the beginning of the century; Beniamino Gigli, who was at the height of his career between the two world wars; and Luciano Pavarotti, who has made himself into something of an operatic 'superstar' on both sides of the Atlantic.

Donizetti poster

Giacomo Puccini

Television has caused a decline in cinema-going in most European countries but in Italy this is not the case. Every Italian town has one or more cinemas and Rome has well over a hundred.

There are three basic types of cinema: the *prima visione* luxury picture houses, which are most expensive and show big box-office attractions when they first appear; the *seconda visione*, which are lower-priced and show re-runs of recent films; and the *essai* cinemas, which are very cheap and show older films but change their programme each night.

All types of film are popular, whether made in Italy or imported from abroad and dubbed into Italian. Westerns, war films, horror films and comedies tend to draw the biggest crowds. Censorship is lax and sex movies are on general release so there is an 18 year lower age-limit on films regarded as unsuitable for youngsters.

The Italian film industry

Given the Mediterranean climate and the wide variety of possible scenic and historical locations, Italy is ideally suited as a film-making country. Rome is the centre of Italian film production and has had many different studios in different parts of the city. Today the industry is in decline and only the biggest of these studios, *Cinecittà* in Rome's south-eastern suburbs, is still important. It mostly makes cheap budget comedy and horror films together with what have become known as 'spaghetti westerns' though occasionally a famous director will use it for something more spectacular. It is generally cheaper to produce westerns in Italy than in the USA and there is plenty of *macchia* scrubland which looks like the landscape of the Wild West.

Italian film personalities

With so much film-making activity, Italy has produced many film stars and directors of international importance. A whole series of actresses who were 'discovered' by Italian directors have gone on to make films in the United States and elsewhere and have become household names. These include Sophia Loren, Claudia Cardinale and Gina Lollabrigida.

Italian directors have had a great influence upon contemporary cinema. This is for various reasons ranging from their realistic approach to everyday life and social 'message' to their use of fantasy and special effects, or often just for their sheer visual beauty.

As soon as the Germans had left Rome in 1944 there was a rush of film-making activity. One of the first major works to appear was a Rossellini's *Roma: Città Aperta* ('Open City') which dealt with the liberation of the capital. Soon after, Rossellini made another important war film *Paisà*. His contemporary, Vittorio De Sica was famous for his 'social realism' films which used non-professional actors working on location in the poorer parts of cities. His finest films, *Bicycle Thieves* and *Miracle in Milan*, were made in the immediate post-war period when poverty was still widespread in Italy.

A typical cinema hoarding

Sophia Loren

Luchino Visconti also started out by making relatively simple 'social realism' films but later went in for more lavish colour productions set in recent historical times. Two of these were *Il Gattopardo* (The Leopard) set in 19th-century Sicily and *Ludwig* set in the sumptuous court of mad King Ludwig II of Bavaria. Michelangelo Antonioni started his career as a film journalist during the war in France and used skills and experience gained there in his films.

More than anyone else Franco Zefirelli has gone in for films which are visually pleasing, yet some would say that his works are too sugary or sentimental. His major films have included *Romeo and Juliet* and *Brother Sun, Sister Moon* based on the life of St Francis of Assisi. Zefirelli also designs sets for lavish operas and was called in by the Vatican as special advisor on the 'staging' of important masses during the 1975 Holy Year!

Federico Fellini has made perhaps the most distincly 'Italian' modern films. His works are full of fantasy, colour and special effects. They range over a wide field of subject matter and are generally very satirical. (He is dealt with more fully in Chapter 59.)

Questions

1 Do you think Italians have a wider choice of films than you do in your country?
2 What is it about the Mediterranean climate that makes Italy ideal for the film industry? What other important film producing area has a similar climate?
3 What is a 'spaghetti western'?
4 What do you understand by 'social realism' in films? Why do you think this type of film was made after World War 2?

33   The Media

Newspapers

Fewer newspapers are sold in Italy than in most other European countries, and more newspapers are sold in the north than in the south. For example, in Piedmont one newspaper is produced for every five inhabitants; in Sicily the figure is one for every hundred.

Many Italian newspapers started up before 1870 and have a strong regional flavour. The two newspapers with the largest circulations are not produced in Rome but in Milan (*Corriere della Sera*) and Turin (*La Stampa*). These two newspapers each sell about half a million copies daily and are highly respected both at home and abroad. Rome has two major dailies—*Il Messaggero* and *Il Tempo*—each of which sells over a quarter of a million copies. These four major newspapers can be found on news-stands throughout Italy whereas the local papers produced in Bologna, Venice, Genoa and Naples are seldom on sale outside their regions.

Italian newspapers have a rather old-fashioned appearance. They are generally large-format, have detailed coverage of Italian politics, sport and the arts but often neglect foreign news. Picture newspapers like the English *Sun* and *Daily Mirror* are very uncommon in Italy.

Some newspapers are purely political in origin: *L'Unità*, for example, is the official organ of the *PCI* (Communist Party) and *Il Manifesto* of an extreme left-wing group.

The main Italian daily newspapers

Man reading the *Messaggero*

Magazines

Newspapers are sold at street kiosks rather than in shops. The kiosks are easily recognizable by their bright displays of coloured magazines.

There is a great range of magazines, from the serious news and cultural weeklies such as *Epoca* and *Espresso* to the more frivolous women's magazines which thrive on gossip about filmstars and the British Royal Family. There are also specialist 'glossies' on all sorts of subjects including sports, science, fashion, holidays, hobbies, pop music and photography. Very popular too are encyclopedias on such things as archaeology and cookery which can be bought in weekly instalments.

Perhaps the most widely read magazines are the small ones which contain comic cartoon strips. These are known as *fumetti* ('little smokes'—a reference to the 'word bubbles' coming from the mouths of the cartoon characters) and are read by people of all ages. *Topolino* (Mickey Mouse) is the most popular *fumetti* character. The *fotoromanza* is a similar type of magazine; it has love stories illustrated in strip-photograph form.

Radio and television

The national radio and TV networks are run by *RAI* (Radiotelevisione Italiana). *RAI* runs three radio channels of which *Radiouno* and *Radiodue* have a mixture of news items and pop music and *Radiotre* has classical music. In addition to these are dozens of private commercial radio stations. Broadcasting from the heart of Rome is *Radio Vaticana*. This transmits news and religious programmes to all parts of the world.

Television has had a much greater impact than radio on the Italian people. It has changed the old way of life and families now gather around their TV sets in the evenings rather than make their own entertainment or chat about the day's happenings.

In Italy it is possible to tune in to a great number of different television stations. *RAI* operates three channels. *Raiuno* and *Raidue* provide a similar range of programmes including crime series from the United States and historical serials from Britain. The main difference between these channels is political. The news of *Raiuno* has a Christian Democrat slant whereas that of *Raidue* has a more socialist bias. *Raitre*, which is relatively new, has more cultural and regional programmes than the other two channels. All *RAI* television has advertising.

Television can also be picked up from neighbouring France, Monte Carlo, Switzerland and Yugoslavia. Swiss programmes from the Ticino areas and Yugoslavian programmes from Capodistria are in Italian.

In addition to the major television channels there are over a hundred private stations throughout Italy and it is possible to tune into twenty or thirty of these in most parts of the country. These channels are all commercial and spend most of the time showing old American and Italian films and 'soap operas'.

A page from an Italian television magazine

Questions

1 Why are the main Italian newspapers regional?

2 Why do you think Italian internal politics get so much coverage in the newspapers?

3 Is the range of magazines available in Italy greater than in your country?

4 Why do you think cartoon strips are very popular in Italy?

5 Is it a good idea to have different political angles to the news programmes on Italy's two main TV channels? (Look back to Chapter 27 on Politics.)

6 Do you think the Italians are lucky to have so many TV programmes to choose from?

7 Do you think that the changes TV has made to family life in Italy are good or bad?

34 Travel and Transport

Questions

1 What are the main changes taking place in the Italian transport system?

2 Why are so many *autostrada* stretches so dramatic to drive along?

3 Why are some Italian trains so slow?

4 Why do you think some ferry boats get overcrowded during the summer?

5 Why do you think the name 'Leonardo da Vinci' is very appropriate for an airport. (If you don't know turn to Chapter 53.)

6 What is the name of Italy's national airline?

7 Why is Rome in such a good position for inter-continental air traffic? (Look at a world map.)

8 Why are internal airlines so well used in Italy? (Think of the country's shape.)

9 What are the problems of getting about in Italian cities?

For further research

Choose one of the types of transport dealt with in this section. Find out how it compares with the service offered in two other countries.

Italy is a nation of travellers. Whether by road, rail, sea or air, for work, holidays or just visiting relatives, most Italians travel long distances during the year.

Roads

The ancient Roman Empire depended on a good road system and modern Italy also has an excellent road network. It is based on the *autostrade* (motorways) and *superstrade* (super highways).

The first *autostrada* was built in 1923, and today there are well over five thousand kilometres of fast, multi-lane highways. None of Italy's major cities is far from this network. The most famous of the *autostrade* is the *Autostrada del Sole* which links Milan to the tip of Calabria by way of Florence, Rome and Naples. Its most dramatic stretch, through the Emilian Apennines with dozens of tunnels and huge raised viaducts, is one of the wonders of modern engineering.

There is also a good connecting network of state roads, many of which are being upgraded to accommodate the ever-growing volume of local traffic. In the South and Sardinia, where roads have been traditionally poor, the *Cassa per il Mezzogiorno* has a very active road-building plan.

Transport

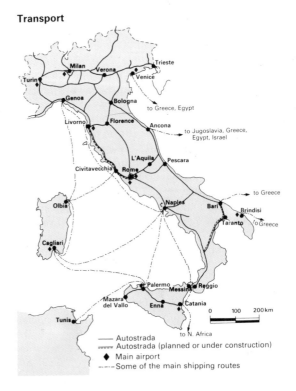

— Autostrada
--- Autostrada (planned or under construction)
◆ Main airport
-·-·- Some of the main shipping routes

Railways

Most of Italy's railways are in the hands of the *F.S. (Ferrovie dello Stato—State Railways)*. This system has over 20,000 kilometres of track linking all of the main cities and also crossing some of the remoter areas of countryside. Trains are often very crowded and this reflects both their popularity and their relative cheapness. Journeys can be slow, however, especially on the many single track lines (common in mountainous areas) as trains have to wait for each other at scheduled passing places.

The main lines are nearly all electrified but many of the smaller branch lines have diesel locomotives. Some of the branch lines are run by private companies rather than the F.S. They include the routes through the centre of Sardinia and around the foot of Mount Vesuvius.

There are various categories of trains on the main lines. The fastest are the *rapidi* and *super-rapidi* which may be non-stop between one large city to the next. Passengers are charged a supplement on these trains. The *espressi* are the ordinary expresses which are fast but stop at the main towns, and the slowest trains are the *direttissimi* and *locali* which stop at every station.

Only three Italian cities have a *metropolitana* (underground railway) and they are not as widespread or modern as those in London, Paris or New York. Milan and Rome both have two lines on their underground and Naples just one.

Sea Transport

The people living on the many Italian islands rely heavily upon sea transport. For Sicily there are the short ferries across the Straits of Messina which take a few minutes, but for Sardinia several hours of travel are involved. The closest sea link to Sardinia is Civitavecchia near Rome. The smaller island groups also have their regular ferries, which can become unbearably crowded in the high summer peak season—when holiday makers are often turned away.

Air Traffic

Italy has several large airports which handle both international and domestic flights. Some of these airports are named after great Italian explorers (such as 'Cristofero Colombo' in Genoa and 'Marco Polo' in Venice). The country's busiest airport is 'Leonardo da Vinci' built in 1960 on reclaimed coastal marshes just outside Rome. This handles ten million passengers a year and is the headquarters of Italy's national airline *Alitalia*.

Internal air routes are important both for getting from north to south and from the mainland to Sicily and Sardinia. The most heavily used internal route is between Rome and Milan and is mainly used by business people.

Traffic in towns

The large Italian cities are crowded and congested with traffic because they lack good underground railways. It can take a very long time to get from one side of a city to another. Most places have cheap bus and tram services with flat-rate fares but they become hopelessly overcrowded during rush-hours. Many people—particularly the young—use *motorini* (small motorbikes and scooters) to wind quickly through the traffic jams and along the pavements if need be.

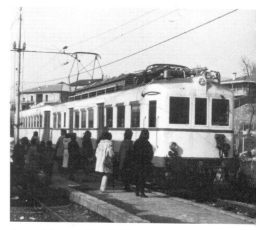

A rural branch line in Tuscany

A crowded ferry in Sicily

Bus and *motorini* in Rome

75

Revision: Section Two

I   What are the following?

motorini   *Terza Media*   *onomastico*   *carabinieri*   *mammismo*
grano duro   *seconda visione*   *opera buffa*   *bocce*   *fumetti*

II   Where would you find the following?

1   Traditional puppets on sale in tourist shops
2   *Cinecittà*
3   The 'Wedding to the Sea' festival
4   A village festival in which a statue is covered in live snakes
5   Italy's main fashion houses
6   TV stations outside Italy which broadcast programmes in Italian
7   *Lacryma Cristi* wines
8   *Marco Polo* airport
9   Cardinals in 'conclave'
10   *Metropolitana* railways

III   True or false?

1   Italy was once known as *Enotria* because it produced so much wine.
2   *Bel canto* is a style of operatic singing.
3   *Vendetta* is another name for a wine harvest.
4   *Asti* wines were 'discovered' and developed by two Englishment.
5   *Capuccino* is named after the colour of a Dominican monk's habit.
6   The *Palio* is a horse race held each year in Tuscany.
7   The *Corriere della Sera* is Milan's main newspaper.
8   *Linguine* are a round type of *pasta*, like *spaghetti*.
9   The Swiss Guard uniform was designed by Leonardo da Vinci.
10   The old ladies of Scanno in the Abruzzi still wear a local costume.

IV   Multiple choice:

1   The *Corsa dei Ceri* is held in Gubbio/Siena/Spoleto.
2   Topolino is a type of cheese/a cartoon character/a sport.
3   *Madame Butterfly* was written by Puccini/Rossini/Bellini.
4   An *osteria* is the first course of a meal/a food shop/a type of eating place.
5   Pavarotti is a politician/opera singer/film director.
6   Monza is famous for its tennis tournament/arts festival/Grand Prix racing circuit.
7   *Carnevale* occurs just before Lent/just before Easter/just after Christmas.
8   UPIM is a trade union/a chain store/a private television channel.
9   *Il Tempo* is published in Rome/Naples/Turin.
10   *Espresso* is a type of coffee/type of train/name of a magazine.

V   Who:

1   directed a film called *Bicycle Thieves*?
2   would work in a *macelleria*?
3   were the two popes who died in 1978?
4   wrote an opera called *The Barber of Seville*?
5   was the Republican Party politician who became Prime Minister in 1981?
6   is said to have brought *pasta* to Italy?
7   would wear a cocked hat with a red and blue plume?
8   was put to death in Rome around AD 67?
9   as a film director is called in by the Vatican to advise how to 'stage' papal ceremonies?
10   was John Woodhouse

VI   What to the following initials stand for?

1   CGIL   2   FS   3   RAI   4   DC   5   PRI

Section three: The history of Italy

35 The First Civilizations

Italy has a central position within the Mediterranean and from earliest times was open to invasion and settlement from all sides. The Etruscans were the first civilized people—or town dwellers—to reach Italy, colonizing the Tyrrhenian coast between the 10th and 7th centuries BC. Their towns, many of which were perched high upon volcanic plateaux, were separate city-states. Groups of city states sometimes banded together when threatened from outside.

The Etruscans had a sophisticated culture and produced a wealth of decorated pottery and bronzeware. They loved hunting, athletics and feasting—themes which frequently appear in their art. But this luxurious living proved to be their downfall. From the 5th to the 3rd centuries BC their towns were systematically destroyed by the conquering Romans.

The Etruscans gave much to Rome, especially in architecture and engineering. Two of the kings of ancient Rome were Etruscans, and the aqueducts, temples, bridges and sewers of the city were built using knowledge and skills acquired from the Etruscans.

The Greeks

Ancient Greece was overcrowded and from the 8th century BC onwards Greeks settled in southern Italy, which became known as *Magna Grecia* or 'Greater Greece'. The colonies were organized into city states similar to those in Greece. They were generally on good terms with the local tribes but occasionally went to battle with the Etruscans. With over a quarter of a million people, Syracuse (*Siracusa*) was the largest Greek overseas colony and was for a time more powerful than Athens.

There were many Greek settlements in south and west Sicily but the western part of the island was dominated by the Carthaginians. These were a constant threat to the Greeks and by the 3rd century BC the Romans were also a problem as they pressed south. Before long the Greeks were forced to accept Roman protection against the Carthaginians as the Punic Wars began (264 BC onwards).

The Greeks, with their opulent culture, left some of their most magnificent monuments in Italy. The most imposing of these are the great temples at Agrigento, Segesta and Selinunte in Sicily and at Paestum, near Naples.

Etruscan tombs: these were piled high with treasured possessions. They contained terracotta effigies of the dead who were shown in the position of reclining for supper.

The earliest civilizations

Questions

1 How would you define '*civilization*'?
2 What were the advantages and disadvantages of hilltop settlements?
3 What is a 'city state'?
4 Why do tombs tell us more about the Etruscan way of life than their towns?
5 Why did southern Italy become known as *Magna Grecia*?
6 From which continent did the Carthaginians come?

Greek temple at Selinunte, Sicily

36 The Rise of Rome

The site of Ancient Rome

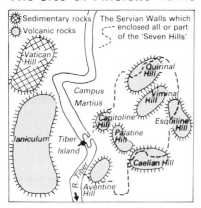

Between the lands held by the Greeks and the Etruscans was Latium, where the Latin peoples lived. They were farmers living in hut villages on hilltops. There was rivalry between the different tribes and they were often at war with one another.

Rome was then a series of villages built on a group of hills close to the River Tiber. It eventually merged to form one large town in about the 8th century BC. The area of flat land under the hills became the place where public business was discussed or *forum*. Early Rome was ruled over by kings. The first of these were popular but the later ones, who were Etruscans, upset the Romans. In 510 BC the last king, Tarquinius Superbus, was expelled and the city became a republic. By this time Rome was already a fine city with its great temple to Jupiter, a thick protective wall enclosing the seven hills and a well-organized water supply.

The expansion of Roman territory

In 316 BC the Gauls, fierce warriors from the north, destroyed Rome, but within years it was rebuilt more splendidly then before. At the same time Rome itself began to extend its influence, either by making alliances or by conquest, and bit by bit central Italy was added to the Roman State. The Etruscans were crushed after long resistance and became part of what was known as the Northern Confederates. The Southern Confederates were formed by various tribal groups and the conquered cities of *Magna Grecia*.

By 173 BC, the Romans ruled all the land which today is Italy. The word *Italia*, which had once meant just the tip of the peninsula, was used by the Romans to mean the whole of Italy.

Republican temple in Rome

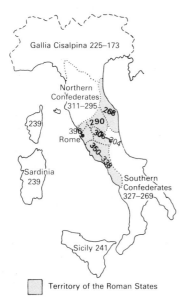

The expansion of Rome within Italy

(Figures refer to dates of conquest – BC)

The Punic Wars

Carthage was a rich and powerful city which heavily taxed its colonies, including Sicily. Sicily decided to ally itself with Rome which did not tax its possessions. This brought Rome and Carthage into conflict and led to the Punic Wars.

The First Punic War (264–241 BC) was fought mainly at sea, and Rome won. The Second Punic War (218–202 BC) was fought much closer to Rome. The Carthaginian general, Hannibal, took his forces from New Carthage in Spain through France and crossed the Alps into Italy. At Lake Trasimeno in Umbria there was a bloody battle in which the Roman army was massacred. This could have been the end of Roman civilization but with grim determination the army was reformed. After heavy losses in southern Italy, Hannibal was driven back to North Africa where he was finally defeated. From then on Rome was the undisputed ruler of the Mediterranean.

Julius Caesar

The politics of republican Rome

In early Rome a few powerful families emerged as a kind of ruling class. They were known as the *patricians*. Their rivals were the *plebeians*, the ordinary people who had equal rights as citizens but were not allowed to hold office. In 287 BC the law was changed and *plebeians* were granted the right to participate in government. From this time on the Roman Republic was the scene of power struggles between the two factions.

In the last hundred years of the Republic, its overseas possessions grew and Rome got richer and richer. A series of popular leaders emerged with either *patrician* or *plebeian* backing. The most notorious of these were Marius and Sulla. Both ruled with the help of the army and ruthlessly butchered any political opponents. Italy went through a series of civil wars between rival politicians, many of whom were generals, and horror and bloodshed became part of the everyday life.

Julius Caesar

Marius' nephew, Julius Caesar, had been appalled at the excesses of his uncle and decided to become a politician who would put matters right. He was an ambitious, rather conceited man but a brave soldier. He was elected a Consul (one of the Republic's main officers) and in 59 BC became military governor of *Gallia Cisalpina* to the north of the River Po. Pompey, who governed Rome at the time, was jealous of Caesar's popularity and ordered him to disband his army. Instead Caesar decided to march south and seize power for himself. The small River Rubicon was the boundary between *Gallia Cisalpina* and Italy proper and once he had crossed it with his army Caesar had reached his point of no return. He entered Rome in triumph, deposed Pompey and went on to add further lands to the overseas empire. From 47 BC onwards he was the unchallenged ruler of the Roman world. However Caesar had his enemies and in 44 BC 60 conspirators banded together and stabbed him to death.

Questions

1 Look at the map of the site of Rome. What are the names of the 'Seven Hills'?
2 Look at the map of Italy. How long did it take the Romans to conquer the whole country?
3 What methods did the Romans use to gain new lands in Italy?
4 What was the main cause of the Punic Wars? Why do you think the First Punic War was fought at sea? (Look at the map in Chapter 35)
5 Do you think life was pleasant in early Rome?
6 What qualities do you think the Romans admired in Julius Caesar, despite his unattractive character?
7 Where might you now find someone holding the office of 'consul'?
8 Why did Caesar have to go on to Rome once he crossed the Rubicon?

For further research

Find out more about the career of Julius Caesar, his military campaigns and the conspiracy to assassinate him.

37 The Roman Empire

Julius Caesar established a new way to govern Rome: by a single man working with the *Senate* (a council of elected men). The ruler was known as *princeps* or 'leading citizen'. After Caesar's death there was yet another civil war at the end of which, in 27 BC, his adopted son and heir emerged victorious to become the Emperor Augustus.

The age of Augustus

The reign of Augustus is seen as a 'golden age' in Roman history. There was peace for the first time in 200 years and the Emperor set about spending money on good works rather than on wars. Rome itself was rebuilt with unprecedented splendour. Augustus was a patron of the arts and supported poets such as Virgil and Horace. He lived a simple, abstemious life and encouraged others to follow suit. But as Rome became more wealthy it supported a large number of idle people who indulged in all kinds of corruption.

Augustus was succeeded by various other descendents of Julius Caesar who were very different in character. Most of them were human disasters. Tiberius, Caligula and Nero, the three most notorious, were extremely self-centred, suspicious and overindulgent in the pleasures of life. It was Nero who in AD 64 ordered a large part of Rome to

Questions

1 The word *senate* comes from the Latin *senex* meaning an 'old man'. What is the connection?
2 How would you describe the character of Augustus?
3 Why do you think the Roman Empire was relatively unaffected by having bad emperors such as Nero?
4 Look at the photograph of Trajan's Column. How effective do you think it would have been in an age when many people were illiterate?
5 Look at the map of the Roman Empire. Which present day countries were then known as Hispania, Gallia and Dalmatia? Why do you think the Empire did not extend further south?
6 *Arena* is the Latin for sand—how do you think this word became applied to amphitheatres?
7 Explain the saying 'All roads lead to Rome'.

For further research

Find out more about Roman building and construction. How did they build roads, bridges and aqueducts? How did they plan their towns?

The Roman Empire at its fullest extent 117 AD

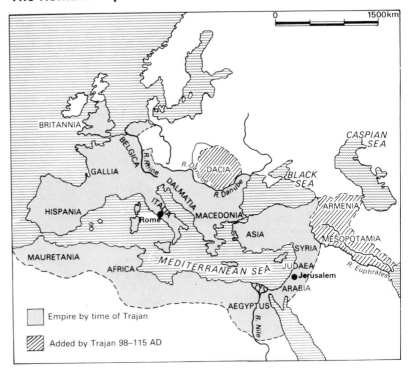

Empire by time of Trajan

Added by Trajan 98–115 AD

be burned and then blamed it on the Christians, giving him an excuse to persecute them. During his reign St Peter and St Paul were both martyred in Rome.

The Flavians

In AD 69 a new family came to power. They were the Flavians and included Vespasian, Titus and Trajan—strong-handed emperors who used the army to defend the imperial frontiers and also to make further conquests. In AD 70 Titus was faced with a revolt from the Jews. He retaliated by destroying Jerusalem. The Empire reached its greatest extent during the reign of Trajan.

The most famous landmark built by the Flavians is the Colosseum. It was the biggest arena in the ancient world and could hold about 75,000 people. All kinds of blood-thirsty spectacles were put on there, including gladiatorial combats, fights with savage animals and, by flooding the arena, mock naval battles.

The city of Rome

Rome was know as *caput mundi* (the head of the world). It was the most marvellous city that had ever been built. With over a million inhabitants and immigrants from all over the vast Empire, it teemed with life. The Forum, with its markets, temples and city offices, was the focal point of the city. Massive public buildings such as baths and theatres were the meeting places of ordinary people. Water was brought in from surrounding mountain regions by a well-engineered system of aqueducts. Rome was linked to every part of the Empire by an excellent network of straight military roads and it was this which enabled the Romans to hold their Empire together for so long.

The Roman Forum

Trajan's Column. This column commemorates the Emperor Trajan's victory in Dacia (modern Romania). Details of the battle scenes are carved into the marble.

81

38 The Decline and Fall of the Roman Empire

Hadrian's Villa near Rome. Here Hadrian reconstructed for his pleasure many of the beautiful things he had seen during his eastern travels.

Constantine the Great

From its height in the reign of Trajan, the Empire underwent three hundred years of decline until Rome was finally sacked in AD 410. There were several reasons for this decline. Many of the Emperors were ineffective rulers, the army found it difficult to maintain the long frontiers against barbarian attacks and, above all, the people were decadent.

Italy had imported grain, wine and other produce for so long that its own agriculture had stagnated and a lot of farmland was abandoned. Many Italians, especially those living in Rome, enjoyed great luxury without having to work for it. The people of the capital had become lazy, pleasure-seeking and corrupt as they lived off the spoils of the Empire. This soft living and the collapse of moral standards made the Romans poor soldiers and the army had to recruit fierce barbarians from the outer provinces to retain its strength.

The Antonines

The Antonine family succeeded the Flavians and ruled Rome for about 70 years. They produced several great emperors, including Hadrian and Marcus Aurelius.

Hadrian was a good administrator who realized that the Empire had grown too large. He gave back some of Trajan's conquests in the East and strengthened the other frontiers with such projects as his famous wall across northern England. Hadrian was an enthusiastic traveller and scholar. He especially loved the Greek culture and spent much of his reign in Athens where he rebuilt parts of the city.

Marcus Aurelius was a refined, philosophical man, very different from the many bloodthirsty rulers Rome had seen. He looked to the East for his inspiration and wrote a book of meditations in Greek. But he was also a man of action and a competent military commander, and managed to defeat various tribes which were attacking the imperial frontiers between AD 170 and 180.

Constantine the Great

The 3rd century was a time of confusion and insecurity. The Empire's German frontier was a scene of constant trouble and there were 24 emperors in quick succession, most of them non-Italian. At the beginning of the 4th century the Emperor Diocletian, frightened by the spread of Christianity, carried out widespread religious persecutions and his successor, Maxentius, continued the anti-Christian campaign.

In AD 306, the same year that Maxentius became emperor, the British-born Constantine was proclaimed emperor by Roman troops in York. In 312 he gathered military support on the way to Rome and, having had a vision of an angel holding a cross, marched into battle behind a Christian banner and deposed Maxentius.

Constantine ordered the toleration of Christianity and put up magnificent churches, including the first St Peter's Basilica, over the remains of Christian martyrs. The Bishop of Rome began to enjoy increasing power over Christians in Italy and was given a large palace, the Lateran, as his residence. Within a few decades, Christianity was made the official religion of the Empire and the Bishop of Rome assumed the title of 'Pope', or father of the Church.

Despite his good public works in Rome, Constantine caused the city great lasting damage. He founded a new imperial capital in the East, which he called Constantinople. The Eastern Empire was economically thriving and safe while the West had stagnated and was frequently threatened by invasion. Constantinople flourished and grew, leaving Rome to become an economic and political backwater.

The fall of Rome

Rome was weak, decadent and unable to cope with the superior forces of the Visigoths who had crossed the Alps and fought their way down through Italy. In AD 410 Alaric the Visigoth leader entered Rome. It was the first time in eight centuries that the city had fallen to foreign invaders. The Empire in the West was finished and Italy was no longer a united country ruled from Rome.

Questions

1 What were the advantages and disadvantages of the Romans having such a large empire?
2 What made Hadrian and Marcus Aurelius different from most other Roman emperors?
3 Why do you think many 3rd-century emperors were non-Italian?
4 Why were many Christian martyrs buried in Rome?
5 In which country is Constantinople and what is the city's present name?

For further research

Find out more about the careers of Hadrian and Constantine. In what ways could they be called great emperors?

Sacking of Rome – Part of stone sarcophagus showing Romans fighting barbarians

39 Italy in the Dark Ages

Alaric the Visigoth's sacking of Rome in AD 410 was followed by centuries of confusion, invasion and foreign rule. Parts of Italy remained attached to the Eastern Empire, ruled from Constantinople, but the vigorous conquerors from the north were the real masters of the majority of the country.

The invaders

The Visigoths found Italy a civilized place and absorbed a good deal of its language and culture and preserved many of the Empire's institutions.

A few decades after their arrival, Italy was attacked by the Huns under their leader Attila who was known as the 'Scourge of God'. They burnt and pillaged towns in the north but were persuaded by the Pope not to destroy Rome.

The next invader was Odoacer, a barbarian who had been a very successful soldier of fortune in the Alps. In AD 476 he pensioned off Romulus Augustus, the last claimant to the title of Roman Emperor, and made himself King of Italy, based in Ravenna. During his rule many public works were carried out throughout Italy, including the repair of roads and aqueducts which had been destroyed or had fallen into neglect. Constantinople tried to re-establish its influence over Italy and called in another barbarian, Theodoric, to overthrow Odoacer. Theodoric paved the way to the Eastern Emperor Justinian's reconquest of Italy and for a short time the country regained some of its former glory.

Ravenna

The town of Ravenna, set in the coastal marshes of the Adriatic, had several times been the place to which Roman emperors moved their court when threatened with invasion. It had the natural protection of the marshes and also direct sea links with Constantinople, from which it could get military reinforcements.

Under the rule of Justinian the city was enriched with many new

Church of Sant'Apollinare in Classe, Ravenna

Mosaic of Justinian and his court, Ravenna

Questions

1 Why do you think the Visigoths and Lombards adopted Roman customs and repaired public works?
2 Why do you think Attila the Hun was known as the 'Scourge of God'?
3 Look at the photograph of the mosaic in Ravenna. How would you describe the people in the picture?
4 Why were the popes of the Dark Ages able increase their influence?
5 To what extent did the lands of the Papal States coincide with those of the old Roman State? (See the map in Chapter 36.)

For further research

Look in an atlas at the positions of Rome and Constantinople (Istanbul). How is Constantinople's position more favourable than that of Rome?

buildings. Ravenna's Byzantine churches which seem rather sombre from their simple brick exteriors are adorned with brilliant mosaics inside. In the church of San Vitale, two groups of highly coloured mosaic figures on a gold background represent Justinian and his wife Theodora wearing bejewelled robes and crowns and attended by priests and servants.

The Lombards

The golden age of Ravenna came to an abrupt end as a new wave of invaders entered Italy from the north. Led by Albion, the Lombards arrived in the Po Valley in 568 and established their capital at Pavia. They ruled for 200 years. Although based in the north, the Lombards managed to gain a few isolated territories in the south. They intermarried with the Romans and adopted many of their laws and customs.

The Church in the Dark Ages

As successive waves of invaders brought greater confusion to the Italian peninsula, the Church increased its influence. The first pope to extend the power of the Papacy was the Roman aristocrat Gregory I, elected in 590. The Church had already taken over much of the commercial activity and administration of Rome but Gregory also saw himself as its ruler, filling the political vacuum left by the emperors. Gregory also made it clear to other churchmen that he, as Bishop of Rome, was supreme head of the Christian Church.

The Papacy further extended its power in 755 when Pope Stephen II produced a forged document granting the Church lands which had been held by Ravenna. Rome thereby came to control Umbria, Marche and parts of Emilia—Romagna. The area became known as the Papal States and was a 'mini-empire' which remained in the hands of the Pope for the next 1100 years.

Pope Gregory I

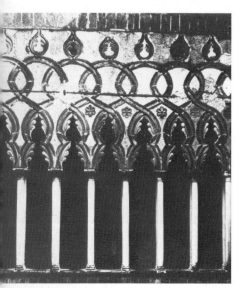

Arabic decoration at Ravello, Campanian Coast

The power struggle between the Papacy and the Lombards had been put to an end in the mid-8th century when Pepin, King of the Franks, captured Lombardy and assumed its crown. The Pope rewarded the Franks with a new title and in AD 800 Pepin's son, Charlemagne, became the first Holy Roman Emperor. This event altered the course of Italian history for it allied Italy to the rulers of northern Europe and left the country open to foreign domination.

The Saracens in Sicily

The Frankish Emperors soon lost most of southern Italy in the confusion which arose from the Saracen invasions. The success of Islam in the Middle East had allowed the followers of Mohammed to sweep through North Africa and during the 8th century they were threatening southern Italy with coastal attacks. In AD 827, 10,000 Saracens landed in Mazara in Sicily from Tunisia and within a few years had overrun the island. Palermo became the capital of a brilliant Arab civilization which lasted for two and a half centuries.

The Saracens carried out raids along the Western coast of Italy and set up small colonies there during the 9th and 10th centuries.

The Normans

In 1015 various Norman knights were visiting sourthern Italy on pilgrimage from France. The south was troubled by warring factions of Greeks, Lombards and Saracens. The Normans offered their services as mercenary soldiers and, after quick successes, were rewarded with grants of land. Within a few decades they became the new aristocracy in many parts of the South.

Robert Guiscard de Hauteville, a brave and cunning knight, welded the whole of southern Italy together as a separate Norman state. Robert's younger brother, Roger, then went on to conquer Sicily, and in 1130 his son was crowned Roger II, King of Sicily. Roger II went on to conquer Malta and part of Libya. His court was a meeting place for scholars from all over the Mediterranean, both Christian and Moslem.

Under the Normans, Sicily flourished. Although feudal, their rule was both just and efficient. The Norman buildings blend the rather heavy Romanesque architecture of Northern Europe with the light and fanciful style inherited from the Saracens.

The Hohenstaufens

In 1154 the German Holy Roman Emperor, Frederick I of Hohenstaufen, entered Italy to unite the country under his rule. 'Barbarossa', as he was known because of his red beard, formed various alliances and fought numerous battles in northern Italy, but refused to go to war against the Norman south. His son Henry married Constance, the heir to the Sicilian throne, and his grandson, Frederick II, became the dominant figure of his age.

Questions

1 Why did the creation of the title 'Holy Roman Emperor' have such an influence upon Italy's history during the Middle Ages?
2 Where did the Saracens come from?
3 Look at the photograph of the Arabic decoration from Ravello. How would you describe this architectural detail?
4 Do you think that Roger II was a good king for Sicily? Why?
5 What does 'Barbarossa' mean?
6 Why did the Sicilians revolt against the Angevins, rather than Arabs or Normans?
7 What are *vespers*? At what time of day do you think the Sicilian Vespers took place?

Castel del Monte, one of Frederick II's castles

Frederick II

The half-Norman Frederick II was southern Italian by birth and upbringing and had nothing to do with his ancestral Germany. He strengthened his Southern Kingdom and many fine castles remain as monuments to his greatness. His court in Palermo was mixed. Christians, Jews and Moslems brought a wealth of invention, learning and literature to the Emperor who was himself a brilliant scholar with wide-ranging interests.

Frederick was always in conflict with the popes of his day. During his reign two marked factions grew up in Italy: the *Guelfs* who supported the Pope, and the *Ghibellines* who supported the Emperor. The names of these rival groups were to play an important part in the future power struggles of medieval Italy.

In 1245 Frederick II was deposed. His illegitimate son Manfred took over the Southern Kingdom but was ousted by the French Charles of Anjou, who was backed by the Pope.

The Angevins

The Angevins, from Anjou in France, were next to rule over southern Italy. They held the southern mainland for over 150 years but lost Sicily very quickly. Charles levied heavy taxation on his new lands and imposed strong military rule which led to a revolt. It was sparked off by an incident in 1282 known as the 'Sicilian Vespers'. A woman was mishandled by French troops on her way to church in Palermo—this was followed by cries of 'Death to the French' and there was widespread slaughter of the foreigners on Sicilian soil. The Spanish House of Aragon supported the revolt and were next to take control of the island.

The Angevins continued to rule the southern mainland with their capital in Naples. They reached a high point with the reign of Robert of Anjou (1309–1343) who was a great patron of artists, poets and philosophers.

For further research

Find out more about the career of Charlemagne. What were his great achievements?

or

Find out about the origins of Islam and how quickly it spread to North Africa and Europe.

or

Frederick II was excommunicated for delaying to go on a crusade and then when he did go, further upset the Papacy by making a treaty with the Moslems and crowning himself 'King of Jerusalem'. Read about the crusades and explain why Frederick's action in the Holy Land would have enraged the Pope.

Palazzo dei Consoli, Gubbio

Medieval Cathedral of Genoa

The City States

While southern Italy was more or less united under its foreign rulers, the rest of the country was in confusion with power struggles between the Papacy, Holy Roman Emperors and other foreign princes. This caused fragmentation, and dozens of cities asserted themselves as independent states.

City life had been highly organized during the time of the Roman Empire and the tradition of people being loyal to their native towns had never died out. After the Empire fell, city folk had to fend for themselves in maintaining their fortifications and public buildings.

Commerce and industry flourished in the better positioned towns of northern and central Italy and they prospered. But they did not always enjoy peace as *Guelf* and *Ghibelline* factions were often at loggerheads, causing disputes both between cities and within them. This explains why many medieval Italian towns not only had strong walls but also defensive tower-houses from which the most important families could fight pitched battles with one another.

Despite the squabbles and feuds, the cities set themselves up as models of good government. The influential people in these city states were professional people such as merchants, bankers, lawyers and doctors. They disliked the unquestioned rule by one individual and wanted a republican system of government with elected civic leaders. The leaders went by different names in different towns, including *consuli* (consuls), *priori* (priors) and *capitani* (captains). Where towns experimented with a single ruler he was known as the *podestà* (from the Latin meaning 'power').

Throughout northern and central Italy there are hundreds of well-preserved medieval cities which still have their walls and old town squares. These squares are dominated by massive, fortress-like palaces,

The republican system was often short-lived as certain families emerged more powerful than others and set themselves up as hereditary lords or *signori*. By 1400 most of the city states had gone this way.

The Maritime Republics

Three of the most prominent medieval city republics were Pisa, Genoa and Venice. They were powerful because they were ports. Pisa and Genoa worked together in 1016 to expel the Saracens from their colonies in Sardinia but then became great rivals for the western Mediterranean trade routes. For two centuries the Pisans had the upper hand but in 1282 they were heavily defeated by the Genoese at the Battle of Meloria. From then on Genoa had supreme control over the Tyrrhenian Sea.

At the head of the Adriatic Sea, Venice had grown up as a refugee settlement and became a city republic as early as AD 697. From then on the city prospered from eastern trade. By 1100 Venice was the main port of the Adriatic and flourished during the Crusades. She gradually colonized Mediterranean islands and for a while held Crete and Corfu. Inland, much of north-east Italy came under Venetian domination. Venice took great advantage of her position between east and west; twice a year 'Flanders galleys' set out taking spices and sugar to Southampton and Bruges and returned with Scandinavian furs, English wool and French wines.

The Papacy and the Papal States

During the Middle Ages the Church had its ups and downs. By the mid-10th century, the Papacy had become discredited because of a scheming noblewoman called Marouzia. The mistress of Pope Sergius III, she was the power behind the throne for many papal reigns including those of her son and grandson. In 1059 a law was passed stating that Popes must be elected by fellow cardinals.

A few years later Gregory VII became Pope. He was keen on reform and wanted to show that the Church was right in its moral judgements. This caused a bitter dispute with the Holy Roman Emperor Henry IV, which ended with Gregory's deposition.

But the high point in the medieval Papacy was the reign of Innocent III (1198–1216). He made himself supreme lord of the Papal States—a belt of land stretching from modern Lazio, through Umbria to the Marche and the Po Valley, cutting southern Italy off from the north.

By the late 13th century, the French were gaining a lot of influence in Italy and often caused deadlock during Papal elections. The most extraordinary of these was the Conclave of 1268 held at Viterbo to the north of Rome. The cardinals were locked away so long that the townspeople stripped off the roof of the palace in which they were meeting. It took two-and-a-half years to elect a new pope!

Between 1309 and 1376 French domination was complete and the papal residence was moved from Rome to Avignon. During this time the Papal States fragmented into city states and there was an attempt to make Rome into a republic. In 1347 Cola di Rienzo set himself up as a popular dictator, but his attempts to unite Italy under a Roman Republic led to his downfall and violent death.

In 1376, the Popes returned to Rome, but it was only with difficulty that they re-established firm rule over the Papal States.

Pope Innocent III

Questions

1 Why did city folk have to fend for themselves during the Dark Ages?
2 Look at the photograph of the medieval *palazzo*. How would you describe it? Is it more like a town hall or a castle?
3 Where in Italy can you find a city-republic today? What are its elected leaders called? (See Chapter 9.)
4 How was government of the city states different from that of other parts of Italy?
5 Which of Pisa and Genoa is today the major port?
6 Why was Venice so well placed for trade?
7 Where is Flanders? What were the advantages of the galleys and the two-way trade?
8 Why do you think there was rivalry between the Papacy and Holy Roman Emperors throughout the Middle Ages?
9 What is a *conclave*? Where do they now take place? (See Chapter 28.)

For further research

Use an encyclopedia to find out about Mediterranean trade in the Middle Ages. Concentrate on the activities of Genoa and Venice.

42 Florence and the Renaissance

Renaissance facade of Santa Maria Novella, Florence

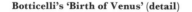

Botticelli's 'Birth of Venus' (detail)

By 1400 Florence had grown more prosperous than any of the other city states. With some 50,000 people it had a flourishing cloth trade based upon woollens and silk, and was the most important banking centre in Italy. Florence had a republican system of government in which six thousand professional people took part. They always adopted a policy of peace to allow the city's trade to function unhindered.

The Renaissance

The prosperity of Florence produced a new leisured class of people who had an appetite for learning. They rejected the education of the monasteries which had hidden away literature by the ancient Greeks and Romans because the Church thought it pagan and unsuitable. The Florentines searched out these books and there was a Renaissance, or 'rebirth', of learning based upon the rediscovery of classical writers. It lead to a surge of interest in art, sculpture, music and science, and the ideal was to be educated in all these spheres, to become an *uomo universale*, a 'universal man'. This Renaissance ideal produced men of genius such as Leonardo da Vinci (see Chapter 53).

The rich Florentines of the 15th century became patrons of the arts and the city thronged with young artists who went there to make a living. Their works were strongly influenced by the revival of interest in the ancient world. For example, the artist Sandro Botticelli frequently chose scenes from Roman mythology as themes for his paintings, and the works of the sculptor Donatello were inspired by the nude statues of classical Greece.

All of this upset the more conservative elements in Florence but the Renaissance had far-reaching effects. Florence became the 'teacher of Europe' as monarchs followed the Renaissance fashions. Italy became the artistic and intellectual model for France, Holland, Germany and Britain (where the 'new learning' reached its high point in the reign of Queen Elizabeth I).

The Medicis

In 1434 Cosimo de' Medici became the most powerful man in Florence and his family ruled over the republic for sixty years. Cosimo was a rich banker who had the finest library in Florence and was a great patron of the arts. Under him there was an architectural revival. New churches were built and elegant palaces replaced the slit-windowed tower-houses of the Middle Ages. Cosimo died in 1464 and was replaced first by his son and then by his grandson Lorenzo.

Lorenzo was himself a man of the Renaissance. As well as a banker and politician, he was a poet, farmer, philosopher and patron of the arts. (It was Lorenzo who first discovered the great talents of Michelangelo.) The personal brilliance of Lorenzo together with the success of Florence during his rule earned him the title of 'Lorenzo the Magnificent'.

Lorenzo died in 1492 and his son Piero took over. Within two years he was driven out of the city by the French.

Girolamo Savonarola

During the Renaissance of Florence a Dominican friar called Girolamo Savonarola had been preaching against what he saw as a revival of pagan living. He condemned the new women's fashions of low cut dresses, the artists' portrayal of nudes and the wealth of the bankers. He whipped up public support with wild sermons predicting that Florence would be destroyed if its inhabitants did not change their ways. He put so much fear of hell-fire in the people's minds that when the French occupied the city, they gave him political power.

Savonarola ruled for four years and led great religious processions in which books and paintings regarded as indecent were burned. However, this religious hysteria did not last long. Savonarola got into a difficult argument with Pope Alexander VI which led to his downfall. In 1498 the Florentines reacted against him and Savonarola was hanged and burned at the stake.

The burning of Savonarola

Questions

1 Why was 15th-century Florence so wealthy?
2 Why do you think the Church condemned various classical works as unsuitable reading?
3 Look at the painting by Botticelli. How would you describe it? In what way might it have shocked people?
4 Why were Cosimo and Lorenzo de'Medici popular with the people of Florence?
5 How did Savonarola get the support of the Florentine people? Do you think that what he did was justified?

For further research

Find out more about the artists who lived in Florence during the 15th century and the works they produced.

List the great English Renaissance writers and artists at the time of Queen Elizabeth I.

43 Rome and the Counter-Reformation

Questions

1 In what ways would Rome have been an unpleasant city in which to live in 1500?
2 Do you think Julius II was a good pope or a bad one? Give your reasons.
3 Why was the Reformation in England different from that in Continental Europe?
4 What was the Counter-Reformation?
5 What is *heresy*? (Look it up in a dictionary.)
6 Was the Council of Trent a good step for the Roman Catholic Church to take?
7 What were the advantages of Pope Sixtus V's building of new streets through Rome?

During the 15th century, Rome had become a very run down place with a high crime rate. Cattle grazed in the Forum and thieves and murderers used the ruins as their hideouts. From 1500 onwards, however, a succession of powerful popes drew artists and scientists away from Florence and transformed Rome into a beautiful city.

Pope Julius II, 1503–13

The most remarkable of the early 16th-century popes was Giuliano della Rovere who took the title of Julius II. He was obsessed with the idea of being the true successor of the Roman emperors and his title was inspired by Julius Caesar. He was a brilliant man of great physical fitness who rode into battle dressed in armour to defend the frontiers of the Papal States.

Julius II is best-known for the rebuilding of St Peter's. The basilica was then over a thousand years old and falling into ruin. Julius wanted the new St Peter's to house his own tomb and got the architect Bramante to design a huge church with a massive dome. It was started in 1506 but took well over a hundred years to complete. The Pope also summoned other great artists to Rome including Michelangelo (see Chapter 54) and Raphael, who decorated the Sistine Chaptel and the papal apartments with their frescoes.

The Reformation and sack of Rome

In Northern Europe, the new learning of the Renaissance was catching on and many were questioning the power of the Roman Catholic Church. In 1511 a young German priest, Martin Luther, visited Rome

The rebuilding of St Peter's

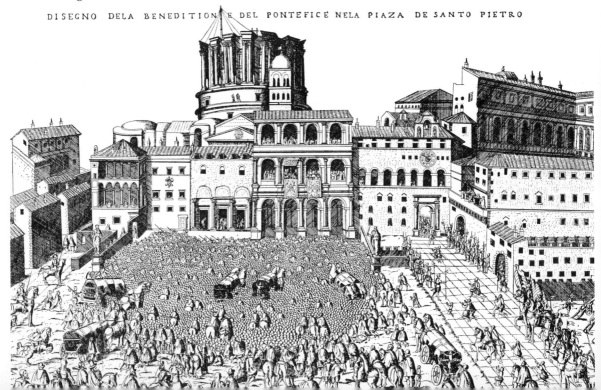

DISEGNO DELA BENEDITIONE DEL PONTEFICE NELA PIAZA DE SANTO PIETRO

and was appalled at how unholy the Church had become and how the Pope was obsessed with raising funds for the rebuilding of St Peter's. Luther preached widely against the Roman Catholic Church and his followers set up breakaway Protestant churches in Germany and Scandinavia. A more extreme Protestantism preached by John Calvin got support in Switzerland and Scotland. In England too, there was a break with Rome, but for different reasons. Between 1530 and 1535 Parliament passed a series of Bills which established the Church of England. This was in retaliation for the Pope's refusal to grant Henry VIII a divorce from Katherine of Aragon.

Within the first few decades of the 16th century the Pope had lost his influence in many important countries. Equally menacing for him were the large Catholic European powers. Northern Italy was held by the French, the south was held by the Spaniards and the Papal States were wedged in between. Pope Clement VII fell out with Spain and in 1527 the army of the Holy Roman Empire under Charles V, which had many German Lutherans in its ranks, attacked and plundered Rome. Amidst scenes of burning churches, looting and rape, Clement and his court were forced to seek refuge in the papal stronghold, Castel Sant'Angelo.

Meeting of the Council of Trent

The Counter-Reformation

In the face of the Protestant threat from the north and the strong pro-Catholic attitudes of Spain, the papacy now set about revitalizing the Roman Catholic Church to stop further criticism. This was known as the Counter-Reformation.

One result of this was the setting up in 1542 of the Spanish-style Inquisition, which tried, and often put to death, anyone suspected of heresy. This led later to the trial and imprisonment of the great scientist Galileo (see Chapter 55) and to the burning at the stake of Giordano Bruno, a Neapolitan philosopher, for his views on the universe.

The positive achievement of the Counter-Reformation was the Council of Trent which met in three sessions between 1545 and 1563. The town of Trent (Trento) in northern Italy was well positioned within the Holy Roman Empire, yet not too far from Rome. Here bishops, abbots and ambassadors gathered from all over Europe. They discussed the laws of the Church, its rituals and its relations with the Protestants. Many religious orders were reformed and some new ones set up. The most important new order was the Society of Jesus (Jesuits) set up in 1534. This was to become the main teaching and missionary group within the Roman Church.

Portrait of Pope Sixtus V

Pope Sixtus V (1585–1590)

Numerous popes continued the work of Julius II in adding to the beauty of Rome, but no one did as much as Sixtus V during his five-year reign. The Vatican Palace was rebuilt, St Peter's dome was finished and a new aqueduct constructed. But Sixtus' outstanding work was in the replanning of Rome. A series of new straight streets were cut through the medieval city to link major churches and palaces, squares were remodelled and new fountains built. The very inventive Sixtus even had a plan to rebuild and roof over the Colosseum to make it into a textile factory, but he died before the scheme could be started.

For further research

Find out more about St Peter's Basilica, its architects and the sculptors who worked on it.

or

Read up about the Spanish Inquisition and how it came to Italy. Did anything like it happen in your country?

93

44   Napoleon in Italy

Italy went into decline during the 18th century. The Counter-Reformation and Inquisition had led to the repression of ideas and many artists and intellectuals had left the country. Italians had little say in their own affairs because most of the country was under Spanish or Austrian domination. Strangely enough it was a third foreign power, France, that changed the whole history of Italy through the invasions led by Napoleon.

Napoleon's background

Napoleon Bonaparte was born on the island of Corsica and was brought up speaking the island's dialect, which is closer to Italian than French. It is not surprising, therefore, that he felt some sympathy with the people of Italy and wanted to do something for them when he became the most powerful figure in Europe.

Napoleon crossing the Alps

The first Italian campaign: 1796

The French Revolution broke out in 1789 and its ideals of freedom and equality spread swiftly among the intellectuals of Europe. Soon hundreds of French spies were in Italy urging the people to revolt.

The other powers of Europe were horrified by events in France. Austria, which held the north-eastern parts of Italy, and the King of Sardinia, who ruled over the north-west, tried to stop French interference, but in 1793 France declared war on them. After three years of struggle, the French, under Napoleon, entered Italy in 1796 and the Austrians were driven out. Little by little Napoleon took over the whole of the country and formed it into a series of small republics.

These republics were short-lived. In 1799 the Austro-Russian army swept the French out and there were wild nationalist risings throughout Italy, often led by bishops and priests. Widespread looting followed the massacre of French troops and towns were set on fire. The old rulers were re-established and sought revenge. Ferdinand of Naples, for example, rounded up hundreds of republican sympathisers and put them to death.

The Italians were disillusioned both with the republican experiment and the repression which followed. Above all there was increasing hatred of foreigners and people of all classes and professions looked towards the day when Italy could be a united, independent nation.

Napoleon's second Italian campaign: 1800–1806

In 1800 Napoleon's army once again came over the Alps into Italy. It crushed the Austrian army at the Battle of Marengo. Within a year Napoleon had control of northern Italy and once again formed it into a republic. In 1804, when he became Emperor of France, the republic was renamed the 'Kingdom of Italy' with Napoleon as king. In 1806 he added southern Italy to his realm thereby placing all of the country under his rule.

Various relatives of Napoleon were given roles to play in Italy. First his brother Joseph and then his brother-in-law Joachim ruled as king of Naples. His stepson, Eugene Beauharnais, was Viceroy of Italy and his son, when a baby, was given the title 'King of Rome'.

The effects of Napoleon's rule

Napoleon fell from power in 1815 after his defeat at Waterloo. Italy had experienced fourteen years of his rule and had benefited greatly from it. There were many new public works, especially roads and schools, but most important of all was the introduction of the French system of administration. The *Code Napoléon* replaced the old-fashioned, complicated and inefficient legal system of Italy and made all people equal in the eyes of the law.

Questions

1 Why did many artists and scholars leave Italy during the 17th century?
2 Why did Napoleon have a special liking for the Italians?
3 Why do you think the European powers feared what had happened during the French Revolution?
4 Why did many Italian people in 1799 look forward to a united and independent Italy?
5 What were the lasting benefits which Napoleon gave Italy?

Napoleon in Italy

45 The Unification of Italy

The unification of Italy

Piedmont
Lombardy (1859)
Venetia (1866)
Parma (1860)
Modena (1860)
Romagna (1860)
Tuscany (1860)
Marche (1860)
Corsica (French)
Umbria (1860)
The Patrimony (1870)
Rome
Sardinia
Naples

KINGDOM OF SARDINIA

KINGDOM OF
TWO SICILIES
(1860)

Marsala
Sicily

0   250 km

■ Territory given to France in 1860
■ Territory gained by Italy
after World War I (1919)
□ Papal States

After the fall of Napoleon in 1815, the European powers met to divide up the lands that France had conquered. The idea of an independent Italy was brushed aside. The foreign rulers were restored to their former positions and Italy was divided into seven states, of which only the Kingdom of Piedmont-Sardinia and the Papal States were ruled by Italians.

The secret societies and Giuseppe Mazzini

From the time of Napoleon's occupation there had emerged various secret societies whose aim was to throw the foreign rulers out of Italy. The membership of these societies included ex-army officers, well-to-do professional people, artists and intellectuals. In the 1820s, new members flocked to these groups and especially to the most famous one, the *Carbonari*.

Between 1820 and 1831, the *Carbonari* organized popular uprisings in different parts of Italy. The foreign rulers reacted by either imprisoning or shooting hundreds of people involved in the conspiracies.

The nationalist movement became better organized in 1831 when Giuseppe Mazzini founded the *Giovine Italia* (Young Italy) movement in Marseilles where he was in exile. Branches of *Giovine Italia* sprang up all over Italy and it replaced the other secret societies. Members paid a monthly subscription and armed themselves ready for guerrilla warfare. By 1833 the movement had over 60,000 members.

Alongside this agitation there was a flood of nationalist literature and a revival of interest in the history of Italy. Poems, plays and operas

Giuseppe Mazzini (who formed movement Giovine Italia)

96

with a strong nationalist content turned the Italians against their oppressive foreign rulers. One such work was the opera *Nabucco* by Giuseppe Verdi (see Chapter 56).

Pope Pius IX

In 1846 there was another event which spurred on the movement for Italian unity. The liberal Bishop of Imola became Pius IX. He freed political prisoners, carried out reforms and tried to modernize the Papal States. But his most radical step was to set up a civic guard, which effectively put guns in the hands of the people. Other parts of Italy quickly demanded similar reforms and to have their own civic guards.

The uprisings of 1848–9

The changes made in the Papal States were followed by similar measures elsewhere. In 1847 Charles Albert, the King of Piedmont–Sardinia, introduced a whole string of liberal reforms at the request of his people including a democratically elected parliament. The following year a rebellion in the South forced the King of the Two Sicilies to grant his subjects a proper constitution.

In 1848 there were revolutions in Paris, Vienna and throughout Germany, and these stirred the people of Milan into revolt against the Austrians. Charles Albert's army was called in to fight the Austrians and a war of independence followed. The struggle ended in 1849 with the defeat of Charles Albert, who abdicated in favour of his son Victor Emmanuel.

Further south Rome had also had a popular uprising in 1848 and a 'Roman Republic' was established. Pius IX, who had proved less liberal than people had thought, fled and Mazzini was established as one of the Republic's three leaders. However, in 1849 Pius IX enlisted the help of the French army who defeated the Republican troops under their commander, Garibaldi. Pius IX re-established his rule over the Papal States.

The Risorgimento 1849–61

Count Camillo Cavour was editor of a newspaper called *Il Risorgimento* ('the resurgence') which championed Italian nationalism. He entered the new Parliament of Piedmont-Sardinia as one of its first deputies and by 1852 had become prime minister. Cavour encouraged the economic development of Piedmont and saw the kingdom as the leading power in a unified Italy.

Cavour knew that another war with Austria was inevitable if Italy was to win independence, so he got on the right side of France and Britain by sending Italian troops to help them during the Crimean War. He had particularly good relations with Napoleon III with whose help he finally went to war with the Austrians in 1859. They scored a great victory at Magenta and the Austrians fled from some of their Italian territories. Cavour annexed the duchies of Tuscany, Parma and Modena to Victor Emmanuel's kingdom.

But this second war of independence ended in defeat for France and Piedmont and the Italian cause suffered in the Treaty of Villafranca which followed. The Austrians remained in Italy and France took Savoy and Nice as payment for their help during the war.

Pope Pius IX

Garibaldi on horseback

97

Count Camillo Cavour

Attempts to unify Italy had so far all been made in the north, but the rapid succession of events which in 1860 finally achieved Italian independence actually started in the south. While Cavour hesitated it was Giuseppe Garibaldi, a Genoese fisherman's son, who took the initiative.

Mazzini had sent his close friend Francesco Crispi to incite rebellion in Sicily. An uprising followed and Garibaldi set out for Sicily with a thousand troops to liberate the island. The 'redshirts', as the nationalists were known, landed in Marsala and within a fortnight had conquered Sicily. Garibaldi claimed the island in the name of Victor Emmanuel and set himself up as temporary dictator. Two months later the rest of the south had fallen and Garibaldi became dictator of Naples.

Before Garibaldi could attack his next objective, the Papal States, the Piedmontese army under Cavour's instructions had occupied Umbria and the Marche, leaving the area around Rome itself (the 'Patrimony of St Peter') in the hands of Pius IX. Garibaldi was considered too powerful and was asked by Cavour to go into semi-retirement.

Plebiscites were held in the South, Umbria and Marche and the people voted overwhelmingly to become a part of the Kingdom of Italy under Victor Emmanuel II.

The Roman question 1861–70

Turin became the first capital of the new Kingdom of Italy but most people felt that Rome was the natural capital for their country and that it should be removed from the Pope's jurisdiction. Napoleon III's French troops safeguarded the territory for Pius IX and successfully fought off the attempt of Garibaldi (who had come out of retirement) to capture Rome in 1867. The final capitulation of the Papal city came in 1870 when France had lost the Franco–Prussian War and found it necessary to recall its troops from Italy. Italian soldiers occupied Rome on 20th September and a month later a plebiscite gave full support for union with Italy. Rome was the new capital, but the Pope refused to agree to any settlement and declared himself a 'prisoner within the Vatican'.

Victor Emanuel II

Questions

1 In 1815 Prince Metternich of Austria described Italy as 'merely a geographical expression'. What do you think he meant?
2 Why did the nationalist societies have to be secret?
3 What is meant by 'guerrilla' warfare?
4 Why do you think that literature, plays and operas were so effective in arousing nationalist feelings? (Why could the Austrians not do much about restricting this type of 'protest'?)
5 What was the great advantage to the various states in having a civic guard?
6 Why do you think Pius IX lost his popularity?
7 Do you know who Britain and France were fighting against in the Crimean War? Why did Italy become involved?
8 Why didn't Cavour want Garibaldi to become too powerful?
9 What is a 'plebiscite'? Do you know another word for it?

For further research

1 Find out more about the 1848 Revolutions in other European countries. Why did they take place and what were their outcomes?
2 Find out more about the career of Garibaldi.

46 The New Nation

As soon as Italy was united it lacked leadership. Cavour had died in 1861, Mazzini in 1872 and Garibaldi had retired to a farm in Sardinia. The new nation had many teething problems; parliamentary democracy was difficult to introduce in a country which had not had it before and elections were rigged. Consequently there was a succession of short, ineffective governments and much social unrest.

Francesco Crispi

Crispi was 78 when he became prime minister in 1887. He cracked down on civil disorder, blamed the Socialists for it and had their organizations banned. He then set about creating an Italian empire.

Italy had already acquired a few ports on the Red Sea and Crispi formed these into the colonies of Somalia and Eritrea. In 1890 he declared Abyssinia (modern Ethiopia) an Italian protectorate. Troops were sent in but progress over the difficult mountain country was slow. In 1896, marching on the town of Adowa, the Italian army was outnumbered and cut to pieces by the Abyssinians. This was the end of Crispi's colonial dream and his political career.

Giovanni Giolitti

Social unrest continued in Italy. There were various bomb attacks and in 1900 King Umberto (Victor Emmanuel II's son) was assassinated. Governments during the next 13 years were more liberal than before and there was some success in solving the country's problems. The mastermind behind this change was Giovanni Giolitti.

There were social reforms during this period. Better housing, health insurance, old-age pensions and full voting rights for Italian men were all introduced under Giolitti's direction. The country was going ahead with industrialization in the north and the problem of the south was being relieved by thousands of people going to work in America. Even empire-building was successful under Giolitti and in 1912 Italy seized Libya from Turkey.

World War 1

Giolitti was unable to form a government after the 1913 election and once again strikes and civil disturbances broke out in Italy. The rest of Europe was uneasy and on the brink of war. Once the war had started, Italy signed a secret treaty with Britain and France which would give her various Austrian territories if the Allies won. These included Trentino as far as the Brenner Pass and the Dalmatian coast (in modern Yugoslavia) (see map on page 96).

The Treaty of Versailles after the war settled most of Europe's new frontiers. However, the rival claims of Italy and the new Yugoslavia to the Dalamatian coast remained unsettled. In September 1919, Gabriele D'Annunzio, a soldier and romantic poet, joined with a group of blackshirted nationalist volunteers. They seized the port of Fiume in Dalmatia and D'Annunzio set himself up as dictator. Within a year, though, a treaty was signed between Italy and Yugoslavia to settle the problem.

Questions

1 Why do you think that parliamentary democracy had such 'teething problems' in Italy?
2 Why did Crispi choose Abyssinia as a protectorate?
3 What were the achievements of Giolitti? Was he a more successful prime minister than Crispi?
4 Why was there such massive migration from Italy to America?
5 Why do you think Italy wanted to extend its land to the Brenner Pass? (Look at an atlas and think in terms of Italy's security.)
6 Why was the Treaty of Versailles unsatisfactory for Italy?

For further research

Find Abyssinia (Ethiopia) in an atlas. Why do you think it was so difficult for an Italian army with 19th century technology to attempt an invasion of that country?

Gabriele D'Annunzio at Fiume

47   Fascist Italy

Questions

1 Why were the Italians disillusioned with politicians after World War I?
2 What were the conditions under which the Fascists came to power? Do you think they met with much opposition?
3 In 1922 the Socialists organized a national strike. What happens during a national strike? How did this one play into the Fascists' hands?
4 Mussolini took a title simply meaning 'the leader' — so too did Hitler. What was his title in German?
5 What achievements made Mussolini popular at home?
6 Look at the photograph of the statues from a sports stadium in Rome built by the Fascists. How would you describe the figures?
7 Why was it necessary for the Italian State to come to some agreement with the Pope?
8 What things did Mussolini do to suppress opposition?
9 Why do you think the Abyssinian Campaign was so widely condemned?

When World War I was over, Italy was left with difficulties. Taxes were increased to pay for the war and prices soared. Unemployment was higher than ever with the demobilization of 5 million troops and strikes continued to disrupt the country. Many Italians were disillusioned by the ineffectiveness of moderate governments and extremism flourished. On the left there were the Communists and on the right a new group under the leadership of Mussolini.

Benito Mussolini

Benito Mussolini was born in 1883 in Romagna. He was the son of a blacksmith who had firm Socialist convictions. After training as a teacher, Mussolini entered politics as a Socialist and soon became editor of *Avanti*, the Socialist newspaper. During World War I he enlisted as a private, rose to the rank of corporal and then left the army because he was wounded. He went back to journalism but now took a strong anti-pacifist line. In 1919 he founded an organization of ex-soldiers known as the *Fascio di Combattimenti*. Branches of the Fascists grew up all over Italy.

Mussolini was fanatical and clever. He convinced the Italian people that he could save the country from disaster.

The rise of Fascism

Italian Socialists were under Russian influence. This put a lot of people against them and also gave political ammunition to the Fascists. Strikes and bombings continued but no government was able to do anything about them. They were blamed on the Socialists, and Fascists went about the country in vigilante groups, smashing up local Socialist party offices and breaking up meetings. Gradually the Fascists took over town councils, and in 1921, 35 Fascists were elected to Parliament.

In 1922 the Left failed to see the dangers of fascism and called a national strike. The Fascists took over essential services thereby giving themselves even more power. In October the Fascists carried out a 'March on Rome'. As they entered the city the King asked Mussolini to form a government–effectively a *coup d'état* had taken place.

The march on Rome

A mosaic with the letter 'M' for Mussolini with a *fasces*. This was an axe and bundle of rods which symbolized justice in ancient Rome. The word 'Fascist' is derived from the Latin *fasces*.

For further research

Read up what you can about the *character* of Mussolini. What were his strengths and what were his weaknesses?

Mussolini's achievements

Mussolini was quick to make sure that his rule was unchallenged. Seeing himself as a latter-day Roman emperor he took the title of *Il Duce* (the leader) in preference to that of 'prime minister'. He established a period of firm rule but many people suffered in the process. Mussolini increased his personal power until he became a dictator. The press was censored and non-Fascist trades unions were eliminated. He banned all other political parties and formed a secret police who jailed or killed opponents of Fascism. He always put the Party and the State before the individual.

Some good things came out of Mussolini's rule. There was a programme of road building during which the first *autostrade* were constructed, there was much new housing for working people in the cities and big new industries were developed. In the country he increased agricultural production with such schemes as the draining of coastal marshes like the *Agro Pontino* near Rome.

Mussolini's most important achievement was the settling of the 60-year-old dispute between the Church and the Italian State. After secret talks, the 'Lateran Agreements' were signed in 1929. By them the Vatican City State was established and once again the Pope became a head of state as well as a spiritual leader. Roman Catholicism was also made the official religion of Italy.

Eager to re-establish the glory of the past, Mussolini encouraged new archaeological excavations. He also laid out a wide avenue through the centre of Rome for his frequent military parades. He was obsessed with physical fitness and set up sports clubs and stadiums throughout Italy. Like so many other things, these clubs had to support the Fascist Party.

The Abyssinian Campaign

Mussolini wanted to extend the colonies overseas, and so Italy once again looked to Abyssinia, the country it had failed to conquer in the 1890s. Mussolini declared war on Abyssinia in 1935 and used aeroplanes, machine guns and poison gas against a poor and backward people who had no modern weapons at all. The war was condemned by over 50 countries and Mussolini became internationally unpopular. At home, however, he announced the fall of Abyssinia to thunderous applause from an enormous enthusiastic crowd. Italy had gained an empire but had lost the friendship of many countries including France and Britain.

Brutal muscular figures representing the power of Fascism

101

Mussolini with Hitler

Mussolini's foreign policy was disastrous. The Abyssinian occupation resulted in various European countries imposing economic sanctions on Italy. This enraged Mussolini and he moved away from friendship with democratic countries. By 1938 Italy was drawing close to Hitler's Germany.

The alliance with Hitler

Hitler successfully invaded Austria in February 1938 and a few months later Mussolini invited him on a triumphal visit to Rome. A year later, when Germany had invaded Czechoslovakia, Mussolini looked around for a country to add to the Italian empire. He picked a squabble with King Zog of Albania and in April 1939 overran that small, weak country. A month later Mussolini signed a ten-year friendship treaty with Germany. However, it was a rather one-sided agreement; Hitler treated Mussolini as an inferior and frequently made moves without consulting him. Throughout the alliance relations between Mussolini and Hitler were uneasy and Mussolini had difficulty in asserting his character over the more ruthless German dictator.

Italy at War 1940–2

In September 1939, Europe was at war. Hitler had invaded Poland, dragging Britain and France into conflict against Germany. Italy decided not to join in but the Fascist press began to stir up the Italian people.

In 1940, when Hitler had successfully conquered Belgium, Holland, Denmark and Norway, Mussolini decided to enter the war on Germany's side.

Questions

1. Why do you think Mussolini admired Hitler so much?
2. Why did Mussolini enter World War 2?
3. Why did the Italians do so badly?
4. Why was Mussolini humiliated by the Germans?
5. What factors led to Mussolini's downfall?
6. What is a *partisan*? Which other countries had similar groups during the World War 2?
7. Why did the Germans set Mussolini up with a new government in *northern* Italy?
8. What is meant by a 'puppet' state?

Italian troops in the Libyan campaign, North Africa

Italian forces were not equipped for the new type of warfare and from the outset they failed. Each time he was faced with a setback Mussolini blamed either the lack of discipline in the army or the incompetence of his generals. Two of his most humiliating failures were in Greece and North Africa. The Germans had to help out both times, further straining relations between Hitler and Mussolini.

1942 – the turning point

Mussolini wrote in his diary that 1942 was the turning point in his career. Dispirited by his army's failure in battle, he went into a deep depression made worse by exhaustion and illness. He was no longer a man of action and lived on his illusions of the past. He also spent too much time with Clara Petacci his mistress, who was unpopular with the Italian people. Throughout Italy there were food shortages, and opposition to Fascism grew as people became tired of what seemed a pointless war.

The fall of Mussolini

In July 1943, after victories in North Africa, Anglo-American troops landed in Sicily. Within a fortnight, Mussolini was dismissed and imprisoned. The Central Fascist Party was disbanded and the new Prime Minister Badoglio went south with the King to join forces with the Allied troops. Italy had changed sides but the Germans were still in the north of the country. They rescued Mussolini from his prison in a ski-resort hotel high up in the Abruzzi and set him up as leader of a puppet Fascist state in northern Italy known as the *Repubblica Sociale Italiana*.

By 1944 it was clear that the Germans were losing the war. As the Allies moved steadily up through Italy, the partisans—groups of anti-Fascist Italian troops—liberated the northern cities of Milan, Genoa and Turin. In April 1945 Mussolini was captured and shot near Lake Como. His body and that of Clara Petacci were taken to Milan and strung upside down in the square for the crowds to jeer at. The following month Germany capitulated and the war, which had done so much damage to Italy, was over.

Mussolini making a speech from his balcony

For further research

Look at books on World War 2 and find out about the battles fought on Italian soil.

49 Italy since World War 2

Questions

1 Why was the Italian economy in such a bad state by 1945?
2 Why do you think a majority of Italians voted in favour of the abolition of the monarchy?
3 De Gasperi had been a member of the Austrian parliament before 1919? Explain how this had been possible.
4 Why was there such a quick succession of *DC* prime ministers in the 1960s and 1970s?
5 What was responsible for Italy's economic 'miracle'? Why did it come to an end?
6 Is a 30 per cent inflation rate high? Do you know what the inflation rate is in your country?
7 Can you suggest why some people resort to political violence and terrorism?

Alcide de Gasperi

Italy was in a mess at the end of World War 2. The economy had suffered both from fighting an expensive war up until 1943 and then from the destruction caused by battles between the Allies and Germany on Italian soil between 1943 and 1945. Even more of a problem was the disagreement between different Italian factions following the legalization of political parties for the first time since 1922. Recent history has been dominated by one political crisis after another.

Constitutional changes

In 1944, a cabinet representing the main political parties came to power to make constitutional changes. In 1946 there was a referendum on the monarchy. Victor Emmanuel III, closely associated with Mussolini, had abdicated in favour of his son, Umberto II and the people were asked if they wanted the monarchy to continue. A majority of two million people voted for a Republic and Umberto went into exile.

By 1947 the present constitution had been decided on: two houses of parliament, a figurehead president and effective power in the hands of the *Presidente del Consiglio* or prime minister. (See Chapter 27 for details of Italian politics.)

The Christian Democrats

In 1945 the *DC* (Christian Democrat) party became the dominant force in Italian politics. One of their leading figures, Alcide De Gasperi, became Prime Minister and when the first general elections were held in 1948 the *DC* got a clear majority. De Gasperi, who was from Alto-Adige, was an able, experienced politician (he had actually been a member of the Austrian parliament before 1919) and led Italy through its important period of reconstruction. His premiership lasted until 1953. No other post-war prime minister has held office this long.

Since then the Christian Democrats have lost their clear majority in parliament and have had to rely on the support of other parties. In the 1960s and 1970s there was on average a change of prime minister every year as no-one could keep the confidence of parliament. This political instability has been one of the main reasons for Italy's weak economy during the last fifteen years.

Various *DC* prime ministers, including Amintore Fanfani, Aldo Moro and Giulio Andreotti, were in and out of power several times during the 1960s and 1970s. The reliance of *DC* governments on smaller parties gradually increased and in 1981 a coalition government with a non-Christian-Democrat at its head (Giovanni Spadolini, a Republican) was formed.

The economic 'miracle'

Despite its political instability Italy enjoyed a period of rapid economic growth and prosperity during the 1950s and early 1960s. Increasing cooperation with other Western European nations, the discovery of rich supplies of natural gas, investment in new heavy industry and agricultural reforms all helped Italy's post-war economic boom to be the envy of other countries. Italy's exports soared and the country enjoyed an unprecedentedly high standard of living while inflation was low. It was at that time that Rome became an important centre of the film industry and a playground for the international rich.

The 'miracle' did not last into the 1970s. Like other European countries Italy has suffered great economic setbacks from the energy crisis, the need to import increasingly expensive goods and from the inability to stop inflation. The inflation level fluctuates from one year to the next but in some years it almost reached 30 per cent. The consequent increase in the cost of living has added to the Italian government's problems and strikes and other types of political action are common.

Terrorism

The most unpleasant aspect of Italy's recent history is the increase of terrorist activity. Political violence is nothing new to Italy but the way in which this new form of violence is organized and how it affects the lives of innocent people is rather different. Two groups of people have been involved in recent terrorist activities, the far Right and the far Left. The Rightists look back to the days of Mussolini and want to restore a strong-handed Fascist-style government, whereas the leftists want a revolutionary Socialist takeover in Italy.

There have been dozens of terrorist incidents in the last twenty years including bombings, shootings, kidnappings, and large-scale robberies. The first really serious one occurred in 1969 when a bomb exploded in a Milanese bank killing several people; this was the work of the Right. The number of terrorist acts then steadily rose for the next few years especially as extremist groups retaliated violence for violence.

In 1978 the leftist group known as the *Brigate Rosse* (Red Brigades) kidnapped and killed the well-liked former Prime Minister Aldo Moro. The event shook the whole world and although followed by a lull in political violence, the two political extremes continue to carry out bombings and kidnappings.

The Mafia

Although terrorism is a new thing in Italy, the lawlessness of the Mafia and similar gangster groups is a much older problem. The Mafia was originally formed by a number of Sicilian families who banded together to protect themselves against rich landowners.

They were involved in a lot of crime and violence in the early 20th century, but were more or less stamped out under Mussolini. Many members of these gangs went to America, where in New York and Chicago such characters as Al Capone became notorious criminals.

Today the Mafia is big business and gets much of its money from gun-running for international terrorists and drug trafficking to Europe and America. In Italy the Mafia and similar gangs are responsible for far more killings each year than are the terrorist groups.

In 1982, in an effort to wipe out the Mafia once and for all, the Italian government sent to Sicily one of its most able Carabinieri chiefs, General Dalla Chiesa. After being there only a few months, his car was ambushed and he and his wife were shot dead.

The Pirelli building in Milan – symbol of the Economic Miracle

Posters and flowers on the spot in Rome where Aldo Moro's body was found

Revision: Section Three

I Who did the following?

 1 Who picked a squabble with King Zog of Albania?
 2 Who crossed the River Rubicon and conquered Rome?
 3 Who was crowned first Holy Roman Emperor in AD 800?
 4 Who sent troops into Abyssinia in 1890?
 5 Who regarded himself as a 'prisoner within the Vatican'?
 6 Who was crowned King of Sicily in 1130?
 7 Who as Pope started the rebuilding of St Peter's Basilica in Rome during the 16th century?
 8 Who led a popular rebellion and set himself up as dictator of Rome in 1347?
 9 Who founded the movement known as *Giovine Italia*?
10 Who as Pope extended his power with the aid of a forged document?

II Fit the events to the dates:

510 BC	The Emperor Nero burns Rome
264 BC	The Sack of Rome by Holy Roman Emperor Charles V
44 BC	The Saracens invade Sicily
AD 64	Napoleon's first Italian campaign
AD 117	The assassination of Julius Caesar
AD 410	The Roman Empire reaches its greatest extent
AD 827	The Etruscan king, Tarquinius Superbus, is expelled from Rome
1245	The First Punic War begins
1527	Abolition of the Italian monarchy
1796	Frederick II of Hohenstaufen deposed
1870	Aldo Moro kidnapped and assassinated
1922	Rome becomes capital of a united Italy
1946	Mussolini comes to power
1978	The barbarians sack Rome

III What were the following?

a *podestà*
the Visigoths
caput mundi
Guelfs and *Ghibellines*
the *Sicilian vespers*
patricians and *plebeians*
the *Carbonari*
'*Avanti*'
an *uomo universale*
Magna Grecia

IV *True or false?*

1 The Etruscans built their towns upon the coastal plains.
2 Carthage is on the north coast of Africa.
3 Julius Caesar was Governor of Sicily before he became dictator.
4 Trajan's column commemorates the emperor's campaign in Egypt.
5 Ravenna became the capital of Italy for a while after the fall of Rome.
6 In the Battle of Meloria, Pisa defeated Genoa and dominated the Tyrrhenian Sea.
7 Pope Sixtus IV built many new streets through Rome.
8 Napoleon was born in Sardinia and therefore spoke Italian.
9 Count Cavour was the first prime minister of Italy.
10 Mussolini was rescued from prison by the Germans in 1943.

V Multiple choice

1 The reaction against the Florentine Renaissance was led by Pope Alexander VI/Girolamo Savonarola/Cosimo de' Medici.
2 The *forum* was ancient Rome's civic centre/imperial palace/main public baths.
3 The *Code Napoléon* was the way in which Napoleon divided Italy up into republics/a system of laws/a division of the French army.
4 Benito Mussolini was the son of a farmer/newspaper editor/blacksmith.
5 In 1860 Garibaldi landed in Sicily at Marsala/Palermo/Mazara.
6 The roof was taken off the papal palace at Rome/Viterbo/Florence during the conclave of 1268.
7 The first capital of the United Italy was Milan/Florence/Turin.
8 Constantine the Great was proclaimed Emperor in Britain/France/Spain.
9 Between 1309 and 1376 the Popes moved to Palermo/Avignon/Vienna.
10 In 1935 Mussolini declared war on Abyssinia/Libya/Greece.

VI Where would you expect to see the following?

1 Hadrian's villa.
2 An ancient arena to seat 75,000 people.
3 Elegant palaces built during the 15th century.
4 A palace used for a Council during the Counter-Reformation.
5 A marshland reclaimed by Mussolini.

Section four: Some famous Italian people

50   St Francis of Assisi (1181 – 1226)

St Francis of Assisi is one of the most remarkable figures of medieval Italy. He came from a well-to-do family but gave up all he had to form a simple religious community. That community has since grown to become the world-wide brotherhood of Franciscans.

Early life

Francis, the son of Piero di Bernadone, was born in Assisi, Umbria in about 1181. His father was a rich cloth merchant and so Francis had a reasonable education.

Assisi was a typical medieval city-state and Francis was taught to be proud of his town and to fight for it when necessary. This happened in 1202 when there was a war between Assisi and neighbouring Perugia. Perugia won, Francis was taken prisoner and became seriously ill. On his recovery he went to join up with the Guelf forces and fight against Frederick II in Apulia—but a dream told him to return to Assisi.

One day in the ruined chapel of San Damiano he heard a Crucifix telling him to 'Go and repair my house which you can see is in ruins.' He rushed home, emptied his father's storehouse and rode off to the nearby town of Foligno where he sold both the cloth and his horse. He returned to Assisi and gave the money to the priest at San Damiano. His father was outraged and brought Francis before the Bishop to explain himself. Francis then renounced his worldly goods and left home to live a simple life in the countryside around Assisi. It was here that he developed a great love of nature.

Foundation of the Franciscan order

Francis had a magnetic personality and, although not a priest, began to preach to the townsfolk of Assisi. He began to attract followers. By 1209 he had twelve friars and went to Rome to get the Pope's permission to form an official religious order. This was granted by Innocent III.

While Francis was alive the Franciscan Order spread throughout Italy and gained over 5000 members. In 1212 an order was formed for women. These were the 'Poor Clares', named after a noble lady of Assisi who was one of Francis' devoted followers.

Later life

Francis of Assisi travelled to Egypt and the Holy Land to spread his teaching. He returned to Italy where he continued to live his life of poverty and prayer, and laid down firm rules for his friars. In 1224, on a mountain retreat, Francis had a vision in which he received the *stigmata*—the five wounds which Christ suffered on the cross. Two years later, almost totally blind, Francis died in Assisi. In 1228 Pope Gregory IX declared him a Saint.

St Francis the poet

Francis also composed many 'canticles' or hymns which were undoubtedly sung within his community. Some of these survive as very early examples of Italian poetry.

Before the 13th century poets still wrote in Latin but when Francis was alive Italian was emerging as a distinctive language. The most famous of St Francis' poems is the 'Canticle of the Creatures' in which he praises God for the things He has created.

> *Extract from the 'Canticle of the Creatures'*
>
> Praise be to You my Lord for Brother Wind
> For air and clouds, clear sky and all the weathers
> Through which You sustain all Your creatures.
> Praise be to You my Lord for Sister Water,
> She is useful and humble, precious and pure.
> Praise be to You my Lord for Brother Fire,
> Through him our night You do enlighten,
> And he is fair and merry, boisterous and strong.

St Francis

Questions

1 Do you think that Francis' father would have been disappointed in his son? What do you think his father would have expected him to do with his life?
2 Why was St Francis so successful in getting his followers?
3 Do you know what a friar is? How is a friar different from a priest?
4 Read the extract from the 'Canticle of the Creatures'. What does it tell you about St Francis' relationship with nature?

For further research

Which are the main religious orders other than the Franciscans? Find out what you can about the lives of their founders and to what extent they were similar to St Francis.

51 Marco Polo (1254 – 1324)

Marco Polo

No other medieval explorer went so far into Asia as Marco Polo. In the twenty-five years between 1271 and 1295 he collected a mass of information about the people and the customs of the East. This had a considerable influence on voyages of discovery during the following centuries.

The travels of Marco Polo

Marco Polo was born around the year 1254 in Venice. His father Niccolò and uncle Maffeo both traded with the near East.

When they realized that the spread of Islam might affect their wealth, the family sold up and went eastwards. Here they managed to increase their fortunes and made friendly relations with the Mongol leader Kublai Khan (at his court in Xanadu in Cathay, modern China).

Niccolò and Maffeo returned to Venice and in 1271 set out again for the East, taking the young Marco with them. They sailed first to Acre in the Holy Land and then went overland through Turkey and Persia, crossing hostile deserts which were the hideouts of brigands. They had intended to go most of the remaining distance by sea, but instead of risking the stormy passage to India went inland through Afghanistan. Malaria held them up here for over a year. Then they passed through the difficult mountain country of the Hindu Kush, from which they found the main Silk Road across the Gobi Desert, and by 1275 they were again at Kublai Khan's court.

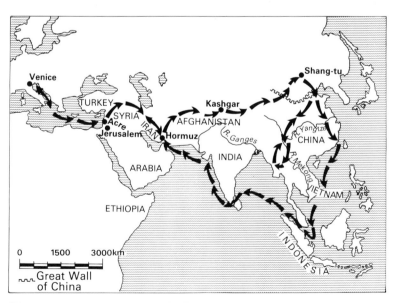

The travels of Marco Polo

For the next sixteen years the Polos travelled around the Emperor's lands. It is uncertain what the older Polos did but they could possibly have been military advisers. Marco, who was greatly liked by Kublai Khan, appears to have held some government office which involved his travelling around and reporting back to the Emperor.

The Polos returned to Italy from Cathay by sea. From around 1292 they sailed through the South China Sea and the Indian Ocean, landing at many different places (and sometimes staying for months). The last stretch of the Asian journey was overland through Persia and into Turkey. From Constantinople they sailed to Venice where their arrival in 1295 astonished everyone who had assumed that they had long since been dead.

'Il Milione'

Soon after his return to Venice Marco Polo was taken prisoner by the Genoese following a battle at sea. Marco had wanted to write up his 25 years of travel but felt he lacked the talent. By chance he was in prison with a well-known writer from Pisa, Rustichello, to whom he was able to dictate his adventures.

The book was entitled *Il Milione* (known in English as the *Travels of Marco Polo*), and as soon as it appeared was a great success. All copies were made by hand and not surprisingly names and facts became altered in the copying.

Il Milione is a wonderful description of Marco's travels with a lot of added anecdotes and sometimes fantasies. The book had a great effect on the people of medieval Europe as it described unknown places in a strange world which was beyond the Moslem lands and therefore difficult to reach. Within a century Islam had effectively cut Europe off from the lands Marco Polo had visited. The explorers of the 15th century were still mainly concerned with finding an alternative route to the East when they discovered the New World.

Questions

1 Why were the Polo family worried that the spread of Islam might affect their wealth?
2 What things made travelling through Asia so difficult during the Middle Ages?
3 Look at the map of Marco Polo's journeys and at an atlas. How many of the world's present countries did he visit?
4 Why do you think the people of Venice were so surprised to see the Polos in 1295?
5 Why do you think Marco Polo found himself in prison with someone from Pisa? (If you don't know look at Chapter 41.)
6 Why were copies of *Il Milione* made by hand?
7 Why did *Il Milione* have such an impact upon medieval Europe?

For further research

Find out more about other great Italian explorers and the places that they visited.

52 Dante Alighieri (1265 – 1321)

Dante Alighieri is one of the most important figures of Western European literature ranking alongside Shakespeare and Goethe. He was certainly the greatest Italian poet as well as a philosopher and political thinker. His major work was *La Divina Commedia* (*The Divine Comedy*) which, written in Italian, had a far-reaching influence on the development of modern European literature away from its Latin origins.

Early life

Dante was born in 1265 in Florence where his family had a few small properties on the outskirts of the city. His early studies were influenced by the old Latin authors and by the scholarly environment of Florence.

Two writers were important to Dante's poetry—his close friend Guido Cavalcanti and Brunetto Latini. Dante, however, developed his own highly individual style which is known as the *stil novo* or 'new style'. He wrote love poetry in the *stil novo* directed at a woman called Beatrice, with whom he never became really close. He saw his love for Beatrice as a mystical experience which took him closer to God.

Beatrice died in 1290 and Dante went into a long period of intensive study. This resulted in the completion of his *Vita Nuova* (New Life) three years later.

Dante with the city of Florence in the background

La Divina 'Commedia' (The Divine Comedy)

La Divina Commedia is divided into three books, *L'Inferno* (Hell), *Il Purgatorio* (Purgatory) and *Il Paradiso* (Paradise). It is modelled on the ancient Roman poet Virgil's epic poem the *Aeneid*. In this the hero journeys through the mythological underworld.

Dante's work is inspired by Christianity and the hero's journey eventually takes him to heaven. Dante himself is the hero and Virgil is his guide through the *Inferno*, but is later replaced by Beatrice who leads him into *Paradiso*. The poem is an allegory of the journey of the poet's soul towards God. Through it Dante wanted to 'remove those living in this life from the state of misery and lead them to the state of felicity'.

Political life and exile

Dante was a fervent supporter of the democratic ideas of the Florentine Guelf party. The Guelfs had held the city since 1266 when Charles of Anjou defeated Manfred, the claimant Holy Roman Emperor. There was still a lot of social unrest in the city.

Between 1295 and 1296 Dante sat on a special council and belonged to the citizens' parliament where he supported laws against the magnates: the richest people in Florence. The Guelfs had split into two. The 'Black' party, led by the magnates, supported Papal power. The more moderate 'Whites', led by the merchant class, supported the Commune of Florence. Dante became a leading figure of the 'White' Guelfs. When they were in power he was an ambassador for a while and then one of the six elected *priori*.

In 1301 the 'Black' Guelfs, headed by Charles of Valois, took power and there was fierce persecution of the 'White' party. Dante had already left Florence and remained in exile; in his absence he was accused of having been a poor administrator and for having opposed the Pope. He and his four co-defendants were tried in their absence and condemned to death.

Dante and other 'Whites' spent the next three years trying to oust the 'Black' Guelfs from power. With Ghibelline support they raised an army but it was defeated at La Lastra in 1304. Dante remained in exile for the rest of his life.

In 1315 Florence granted an amnesty for political exiles but Dante was not included in it. In 1318 he settled down in Ravenna where he wrote his main work, *La Divina Commedia*. In 1321 he contracted malaria and died shortly after finishing the third book of *La Divina Commedia*.

Questions

1 How was Dante involved in politics?
2 How much of his life did he spend in exile?
3 Who were the Guelfs and Ghibellines? (See Chapters 40 and 41)
4 Why do you think Dante supported the 'White' rather than 'Black' Guelf party? (Think of his family background.)
5 How do you think Dante would have removed people from the 'state of misery and lead them into the state of felicity' by writing the *La Commedia*?
6 Why was it easy to catch malaria in Ravenna? (Look at Chapters 9 and 39 if you don't know.)

Illustration from *l'Inferno*

53 Leonardo da Vinci (1452 – 1519)

Leonardo: Self-portrait

Of all the great Italians of the Renaissance, Leonardo was the most outstanding. More than anyone he displayed the qualities of the *uomo universale*, the idealized Renaissance man with wide-ranging talents and interests.

As both artist and scientist, Leonardo's genius was applied to painting, sculpture, architecture and engineering. His scientific notebooks are as important as his great paintings.

Early life

Leonardo was born in 1452 in the small Tuscan hill town of Vinci. He was the illegitimate son of a middle-class Florentine man and a local peasant girl. He grew up in his father's house and received the usual elementary education of all rich Florentines in those days. At the age of fifteen he was apprenticed to the art and technical workshop of Andrea del Verrocchio. In 1472 he was accepted by the painters' guild of Florence.

Leonardo's time in Milan

Between 1482 and 1499 and again between 1506 and 1513, Leonardo spent some of his most productive time in Milan. He entered the service of Ludovico Sforza, Duke of Milan, as 'painter and engineer to

The Last Supper

Questions

1 Why do you think Leonardo found Milan more stimulating than Florence?
2 Look at the *Last Supper* picture. How would you describe the composition of this painting?
3 Why can Leonardo be described as an *uomo universale*?
4 Why do you think Leonardo was a lonely person?
5 Can you think of another reason why Leonardo might have written in 'mirror script'?

the duke'. Here in Sforza's stimulating and brilliant court, Leonardo felt at home. He painted, designed elaborate court festivals, acted as a military adviser on fortifications and worked on various mechanical engineering schemes.

Leonardo's greatest paintings during his Milan years were two versions of the *Virgin of the Rocks* and the vast wall painting of the *Last Supper*. He had many apprentices and students in his workshops but was so busy that there were many projects he never completed. He also devoted much time to his scientific studies and the years up until 1499 were when he was most active on his notebooks.

In 1499 Ludovico fell from power and Leonardo had to leave Milan. He went first to Mantua then to Venice and eventually returned to his native Florence for a while. Always restless and wanting adventurous work, in 1502 Leonardo entered the service of Cesare Borgia, the notorious son of Pope Alexander VI. He travelled with Borgia as a military adviser to the papal army. In Florence he worked on a scheme to build a canal between the city and the sea, and on several paintings. The famous *Mona Lisa* portrait was painted in 1503.

In 1506, Leonardo was back in Milan. The French were in control then and proved to be generous patrons.

His last years

In 1513, the French were thrown out of Milan and so Leonardo moved again. He went first to Rome where the popes gave him their patronage, and he worked on many different projects. Few of these were finished. The ageing Leonardo became embittered as he saw other artists such as Raphael and Michelangelo getting the important papal commissions.

Lonely and dissatisfied, Leonardo took up the invitation of the young King Francis I of France to become 'painter, architect and mechanic' at the summer palace at Amboise. It was here that he died in 1519.

Leonardo's notebooks

During his lifetime Leonardo produced thousands of pages of closely written notes and diagrams on a wide range of artistic and scientific topics. His diagrams included architectural drawings, maps and plans, pictures of his mechanical inventions and extremely detailed biological drawings.

As well as being beautifully illustrated the notebooks have a fine but strange writing. Leonardo used 'mirror script' (the notes could only be read in a mirror) partly for reasons of secrecy and partly because he did not intend them for a wide readership.

For further research

Find out more about Leonardo's experiments and notebooks. Make a list of the machines and types of engineering schemes be proposed.

Design for a flying machine from one of Leonardo's notebooks

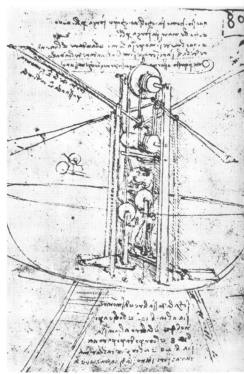

54 Michelangelo Buonarroti (1475 – 1564)

Michelangelo Buonarroti was one of the greatest artists of all time. Like Leonardo da Vinci he grew up in the environment of the Florentine Renaissance and was a man of many talents.

Early life

Michelangelo was born in 1475 at Caprese near Arezzo in Tuscany. His father Lodovico had come from a family of bankers and at the time of Michelangelo's birth was mayor of Caprese. The family soon moved back to their original home, Florence, where Michelangelo received his education. At the age of 13, he was apprenticed to the successful painter Ghirlandaio, and a few years later studied sculpture under the patronage of the de' Medici family.

In 1494, when the fanatical Savonarola took power in Florence and condemned the artists of the Renaissance, Michelangelo fled to Bologna and two years later went to Rome. A man of simple tastes he found Rome corrupt and materialistic—yet it was a place where he could get artistic commissions. In 1498 he completed his first major work, the beautiful *Pietà* which is today inside St Peter's Basilica. Three years later he was back in Florence where he sculpted the gigantic statue of *David*. This won immediate praise and was taken by the Florentines as the symbol of their city's strength.

Michelangelo and the popes

Michelangelo spent most of his creative career in Rome. In 1503 Julius II summoned him to the Vatican where Michelangelo stayed for the next ten years.

The relationship between artist and pope, however, was not an easy one. They had frequent rows, with Michelangelo often refusing to do what Julius asked and consequently not getting paid. Julius II wanted Michelangelo to sculpt a huge tomb for him. It was to have over 40 life-size figures and to be the centrepiece of the new St Peter's. The tomb was never completed because of finances, quarrels, tantrums and the Pope's frequent changes of plan.

One such change of plan was for Michelangelo to leave work on the tomb to paint frescoes in the Sistine Chapel (recently built by Julius II's uncle when he had been Pope Sixtus IV). Michelangelo was not pleased as he regarded himself as a sculptor rather than a painter. Between 1508 and 1512 he worked high on a scaffolding painting powerful Old Testament scenes on the ceiling of the Sistine Chapel.

Between 1514 and 1534 Michelangelo worked a lot in Florence. This was because two of the popes during that period were Medicis and wanted works carried out in their home city.

The Last Judgement

In 1534, Michelangelo returned to Rome for good. Pope Paul III set him to work on the remaining wall of the Sistine Chapel where he produced what many regard as the greatest masterpiece of his

Statue of David

career—the vast fresco of the *Last Judgement*. Much of what Michelangelo painted there was inspired by the religious poetry of Dante—of whom he was a great admirer.

It is an awesome painting with bulky muscular human figures either being saved in heaven or sent down into the horrific depths of hell. In the centre is Christ with his arm raised in judgement. The fresco was unveiled in 1541 and immediately acclaimed as a masterpiece. But it was not to remain quite as Michelangelo painted it. The nudity shocked various popes and cardinals and in 1559 loincloths were painted on many of the figures.

Final Years

In his later life, when he found it difficult to work with hammer and chisel, Michelangelo concentrated on architecture. In 1546 he redesigned the square on the Capitoline Hill in Rome and between 1557 and 1558 designed the dome for the new St Peter's. He died from a stroke in 1564.

The pope would have liked the famous artist to have been buried in Rome, but Michelangelo wanted his remains to be returned to Florence. They were secretly taken back there and interred in the Church of S. Croce, where many other great Florentines were buried.

Michelangelo

The Last Judgement, **Sistine Chapel (detail)**

Questions

1 Was the environment in which Michelangelo grew up a good one for artists?
2 Who were Michelangelo's main patrons?
3 Why was it wise of Michelangelo to flee Florence in 1494?
4 What does the planned tomb of Julius II tell us about the Pope's character?
5 Look at the picture of Michelangelo's Sistine Chapel fresco. How would you describe the figures in it?
6 Why do you think the *Last Judgement* was immediately hailed as a masterpiece?

Galileo was one of Italy's greatest scientists. Brought up in the liberal atmosphere of the Renaissance he went on to make important discoveries in the fields of physics and astronomy. His views, however, brought him into conflict with the Church. He was tried by the Inquisition and spent the last years of his life under house arrest.

Galileo

The leaning tower of Pisa

Early life

Galileo Galilei was born in Pisa in 1564. He was the son of a musician and was educated at a monastery near Florence. He went to study medicine at Pisa University, but one day in the cathedral made some observations about a swinging lamp and its movements which turned his interests to mathematics. He returned to Florence for a while where he published his theories about gravity. Then, on the strength of this work, he went back to Pisa to take up a lecturing post. It was there that he carried out various experiments with weights and pendulums from the cathedral's Leaning Tower. One of the most important things that he proved was that objects of different weights all fall at the same speed.

Galileo and his telescopes

In 1592 Galileo became professor of mathematics at Padua University. He was there for eighteen years and carried out much important astronomical research. He was already convinced that the Polish scientist Copernicus was right about the planets revolving around the Sun, rather than the Earth being the centre of the universe which was commonly believed at the time.

The telescope was invented in 1609. Galileo lost no time in going to the glassworks in Venice to ask the craftsmen to make the first large telescope for astronomical use. In 1610 he announced various observations he had made about the Moon, the phases of Venus and the satellites of Jupiter. What he saw through his telescopes confirmed his belief that the Copernican system was right. His findings caused great excitement in the academic world and he went back to his native Tuscany to become the 'first philosopher and mathematician' to the Grand Duke.

Galileo and the Inquisition

In 1611 Galileo went to Rome to demonstrate his telescope at the papal court. The visit was a great success and Galileo went on to make new discoveries and to publish them.

Meanwhile the Inquisition was examining the Copernican system and Dominican preachers were openly condemning Galileo for his support of Copernicus. In 1616 a decree came out declaring the Copernican system wrong and contrary to the teaching of the Bible. Galileo went into a kind of voluntary retirement for the next seven years. Further researches made him even more convinced that he was right about the Earth not being the centre of the universe.

When his old friend and admirer Maffeo Barberini became Pope Urban VIII, Galileo went to Rome to try and get the decree against the Copernican system removed. He was unsuccessful and returned to Tuscany where in 1632 he brought out his greatest written work. This was a discussion of the two systems—the Copernican one which he supported and the Ptolomeic one which was generally accepted by the Church. The Jesuits were angry with Galileo and felt that his ideas could have dangerous consequences for the Church.

It seems likely that Galileo was the victim of a 'frame up', for certain documents were 'discovered' which enabled the Inquisition to try him for heresy. In 1634, and despite his illness, he was summoned to Rome for trial. After a rigorous cross-examination Galileo was found guilty of holding and teaching the ideas of Copernicus. He was ordered to declare publicly that he was wrong, and he did so.

The Inquisition sentenced him to imprisonment but the Pope changed it to house arrest because of Galileo's age and illness. In 1633 he returned to his little estate at Arcetri where he remained until his death in 1642. Throughout this period of exile he was extremely active with his experiments and scientific writings, and continued to use his telescopes until 1637 when he became blind.

Questions

1 Why do you think the Leaning Tower of Pisa was an ideal place for pendulum experiments?
2 Why did the Inquisition condemn the Copernican system of the universe?
3 Do you think Galileo was fairly treated?
4 Why was the Pope lenient towards Galileo?

For further research

Find out more about the life of Copernicus and see how it compares with that of Galileo.

Galileo demonstrating his telescope

56 Giuseppe Verdi (1813 – 1901)

Verdi

Giuseppe Verdi is Italy's most outstanding operatic composer and transformed Italian opera during his very active career. As well as producing 27 operas and other musical works, Verdi was a great patriot and was closely associated with the movement for Italian unification.

Early life

Verdi came from a very humble background. He was born in 1813 at Le Roncole, a village near Busseto in the Duchy of Parma (which was at that time under Napoleon's rule). His father kept a tavern and grocery shop and could not afford to give the young Giuseppe a good education. A rich merchant from Busseto noticed his musical talent, however, and helped him in his studies.

At the age of eighteen, Verdi was sent to study music at Milan for three years. In 1834 he returned to Busseto to become the commune's musical director, and two years later he married Margherita Barezzi, his patron's daughter.

Early career and Italian nationalism

In 1836 an opportunity arose for Verdi to compose an opera so he returned to Milan. It was called *Oberto, Conte di San Bonifacio* and was performed at the *Teatro alla Scala (La Scala)* in 1839. It was sufficiently well received for other commissions to follow.

His first real success came in 1842 with the production of *Nabucco*, based on an account of the Jews in captivity in Babylon. This story really fired the imagination of Verdi who regarded the Italians as 'captives' of the Austrians. The opera was a resounding success both for Verdi and for the nationalist cause.

In 1840 Verdi had lost his first wife but Giuseppina Strepponi, one of the singers in *Nabucco*, took pity on him. After a long affair they married in 1859.

Soon after *Nabucco*, Verdi produced more operas which served the nationalist cause, including *I Lombardi* (The Lombards) and *Giovanna d'Arco* (Joan of Arc). They passed the Austrian censors because the patriotic message was well disguised by the operas being set in a much earlier historical period.

At the height of the movement for Italian independence Verdi's very name was used as a political slogan. *VIVA VERDI!* was daubed over walls in the Austrian-occupied territories. The slogan did not really mean 'Long live Verdi'; the composer's name contained the initials of *Vittorio Emanuele Re d'Italia* (Victor Emmanuel, King of Italy).

Verdi went on in the 1850s to produce some of his great masterpieces including *Macbeth*, based on Shakespeare's play, *La Traviata* and *Rigoletto*. *Rigoletto* got Verdi into trouble as it contained the attempted murder of a king and a curse, both items to which the censors objected. Verdi had trouble with censorship again in 1859 with *Un Ballo in Maschera* (A Masked Ball). The plot involved the assassination of the

King of Sweden, which the Austrian censors claimed could have incited the Italian people against their foreign rulers. Verdi merely altered the setting of the opera.

In 1860 Italy was unified and censorship was no longer a problem. As one of the great artists behind the Risorgimento, Verdi was persuaded by Cavour to take a seat in the new Parliament in Turin. Verdi stayed for just a year until Cavour's death, after which he resigned.

Verdi's later career

Verdi had become a composer of international repute. He represented Italy at the London Exhibition in 1862 and had new operas performed in St Petersburg in Russia and then in Paris. But his most amazing international assignment came in 1871. He produced *Aida*, based on a story set in ancient Egypt, in Cairo to celebrate the opening of the Suez Canal.

For the last thirty years of his life, Verdi's operatic output was slow. However, many people claim that his best works belong to this period. He was particularly concerned with taking opera beyond just a string of tunes into a more complete music-drama form. He found much good dramatic material in Shakespeare and two of his later operas were *Otello* and *Falstaff*.

In his last years Verdi gave up writing opera in favour of sacred pieces for choirs. In 1897 he suffered the great blow of Giuseppina's death and his health deteriorated until his death in 1901.

Scene from *Aida*

Questions

1 Do you think that Verdi was fortunate to find a patron? Would he have otherwise had a musical education?

2 Why did Austria impose censorship on Northern Italy? How did Verdi overcome censorship?

3 Why do you think Verdi was not particularly interested in his seat in Parliament?

4 Why was the opening of the Suez Canal such an important event in the 19th century?

5 What is there in Shakespeare's plays that would have pleased Verdi?

For further research

Find a recording of *Nabucco* and listen to the 'Slave's Chorus'. Do you agree that this is a very stirring piece of music? What effect do you think it might have had on Italians in the 1840s?

Listen to any other work of Verdi and see what you think of it.

57 Guglielmo Marconi (1874 – 1937)

Questions

1 Why do you think people did not readily accept Marconi's discoveries?
2 Why was wireless communication between ships so useful?
3 How did Marconi change the world?
4 What do you think was Marconi's greatest achievement?

For further research

Find out about the commercial development of radio.

Marconi was one of Italy's greatest physicists and one of the world's pioneers of radio. His life was devoted to improving wireless communications, for which he received many honours.

His early life

Guglielmo Marconi was born in Bologna in 1874 to an Italian father and an Irish mother. He showed an interest in physics from an early age and was educated at technical school in Livorno. At the age of twenty he carried out simple experiments with the transmission of concentrated radio waves, but few people showed interest in what he was doing.

Discouraged, he went to England in 1896 where he became assistant to the chief engineer of the post office. In the same year he aroused great interest and excitement among the British public by transmitting radio waves 16 km across the Bristol Channel.

Development of radio communications

Following his success in Britain and with the financial help of his cousin, Marconi set up his Wireless Telegraph and Signal Company in 1899. At first the company was involved in radio communications between ships and soon the American Marconi Company was founded.

Marconi's great breakthrough came in 1901 when signals from Cornwall were received on the other side of the Atlantic in Newfoundland, providing that the curvature of the earth did not affect radio waves.

In 1909 Marconi received the Nobel Prize for Physics, and a year later extended the range of radio wave reception to the 9000 km between Argentina and Ireland. By furthering his knowledge of radio waves and continually improving his equipment, Marconi gradually increased the distance over which radio communication was possible. In 1918 he sent the first radio message between Britain and Australia.

During the 1920s and early 1930s Marconi's experiments centred around improving reception. This led to the development of short-wave radio. The Marconi Company was then responsible for setting up communications links between Britain and the Commonwealth.

Marconi became President of the Royal Italian Academy in 1930 and died in Rome in 1937.

Marconi's wireless telephone

58 Carlo Levi (1902 – 1975)

Carlo Levi was a doctor, writer and painter who won international acclaim with his documentary novel *Cristo si è fermato ad Eboli* (*Christ stopped at Eboli*) which was published in 1947.

Levi was born in Turin in 1902 where he qualified as a doctor and established himself as a painter in the 1920s. He became an outspoken critic of Fascism and was regarded by Mussolini as a political enemy. Levi's opposition to the invasion of Abyssinia resulted in his being put into exile in 1935. As with other political prisoners of Fascism he was sent to a small isolated village in the South where he was placed under village arrest under close supervision of the local *Carabinieri*.

Levi was exiled to a place called Aliano in Basilicata, the poorest region of Italy, and was horrified by the people's living conditions. His year spent at Aliano was the basis for his book *Christ Stopped at Eboli*.

Levi's writing

Because of their way of life the villagers of Aliano regarded themselves as a sub-human race living more like beasts of burden than human beings. They felt that civilized life and the influence of Christianity had never really reached their part of Italy and there was a local saying that 'Christ stopped short of here, at Eboli.' (Eboli was a town on their road to Naples.)

Aliano (which Levi calls Gagliano in his book) is in the poor hill country of Basilicata (see Chapter 15). It was deforested centuries ago and in the 1930s most of the land was put under wheat by the rich landowners although the soils were not favourable for it. No one invested money in the area and the State neglected it—the State which to the peasants was 'more distant than heaven and far more of a scourge, because it was always against them'. The climate just made things worse with long periods of summer drought and torrential rain during winter causing frequent landslides. On top of all this malaria was still rife in the 1930s and affected a large percentage of the village people.

The villagers themselves had been beaten into submission by these difficult conditions and, as Levi describes them, 'they all seemed alike, short, suntanned with dull, expressionless black eyes like the empty windows of a dark room'. They were a suspicious and superstitious people who feared outsiders and went in for certain pagan practices—such as making love potions. (Levi on his arrival at Aliano was warned to avoid being entertained by women because of these potions!) Any person who really wanted to get on in life left the village for cities such as Naples and Rome, or America. Many of the villagers had gone to the United States in the 1920s to seek their fortunes.

When Levi left Aliano in 1936 it was a very emotional parting. Those who had at first been suspicious of him did not want him to go partly because of his medical skills.

Levi wrote up his experiences in Aliano between 1943 and 1944 in Florence where he later became a political journalist. After the success of *Cristo si è fermato ad Eboli* he went on to write various other books including *Paura della libertà* (*Of Fear and Freedom* in English) which is about the need for intellectual freedom. His later life was devoted mainly to painting. Carlo Levi died in 1975.

Carlo Levi—a statue recently erected at Aliano.

Questions

1 What is 'village arrest'? Do you think it a humane way of dealing with political prisoners?
2 Why were conditions so difficult for the peasants of Aliano?
3 Why do you think Levi changed the name of the village in his book?
4 Do you think Levi's description of the villagers is an effective one? What does it tell you about the people of Aliano?
5 Why do you think the people were sad to see him go?

59   Federico Fellini (1920 –   )

Federico Fellini still from *Roma*

Fellini is one of the most important figures in contemporary Italian cinema. His films are visually very powerful and full of fantasy. Much of his subject matter stems from things in his childhood such as his family, the Catholic boarding school he attended and his early fascination with circuses and the theatre.

Federico Fellini was born in the Adriatic resort of Rimini in 1920, the son of a food salesman. He was fed up with the rather dull way of life in Rimini and in 1938 went to Florence where he worked as a cartoonist for various magazines. In 1939 he moved to Rome where he made money by selling his cartoons in restaurants. Then in 1940 he became editor of *Marc'Aurelio*, a satirical weekly magazine, and three years later started writing scripts for the radio. In 1943 he wrote for the actress Giulietta Masina, who became his wife in the same year. Soon after the Allied forces entered in Rome in 1944, Fellini became a friend of the film director Roberto Rossellini and helped him make *Roma: Città Aperta* (known as 'Open City' in English). Fellini became obsessed with the cinema and continued to work with Rossellini on his next few films.

In 1950 Fellini was the co-director of *Luci del Varietà* a story about a girl who leaves home to become a star in the variety theatre. It was one of many films in which his wife appears.

Fellini's films

Fellini's first major success came in 1953 with *I Vitelloni* and portrays the idle way of life of young men in a typical Italian provincial town. The film, which won an award at the Venice Film Festival, shows Fellini's great talent for making fun of certain aspects of the Italian lifestyle.

In 1960 Fellini produced *La Dolce Vita* which is perhaps his most famous film. It is all about the Rome jet-set of that time and shows the lives of film stars, television personalities, artists and aristocrats who are ruthlessly pursued by journalists and press-photographers. For the film Rome's most expensive restaurant and shopping street, the Via Veneto, was entirely reconstructed in the studios.

Fellini's next two films *Otto e mezzo* ($8\frac{1}{2}$) and *Giulietta degli Spiriti* (Juliet of the Spirits) explore an incredible fantasy world. 'Giulietta' is played by Fellini's wife who gives her name to the title.

In 1969 Fellini worked on a completely new subject—ancient Rome. The film *Satyricon* is based upon the Roman writer Petronius' story of the same name. Many historical films make ancient Rome appear tidy and clinical, but Fellini shows all the squalor and decadence of the city.

The films *Roma* and *Amarcord*, which Fellini produced in 1972 and 1973, are full of the atmosphere of the places in which they are set and are very amusing. *Roma* deals with life in Rome both when Fellini first arrived there in 1939 and in 1972. There are scenes of noisy families having a restaurant meal in the streets, a fashion parade of ecclesiastical costumes (including bishop's outfits with flashing lights!), enormous traffic jams and a motorbike 'burn-up' around the Colosseum (which Fellini reconstructed in the studios). *Amarcord* takes place in an Adriatic resort town in the 1930s and borrows much from Fellini's childhood. It particularly satirizes the morals of a Catholic education and the Fascist régime.

In 1976 Fellini's *Casanova* appeared. This is a long and very expensive film based on the life of the famous 18th-century Venetian lover. The film is full of colour and fantasy with an especially clever use of special effects such as in one scene which reconstructs the Grand Canal and Rialto bridge during a firework display.

Prova d'Orchestra ('Orchestral Rehearsal'), which Fellini directed in 1979, is a very different sort of film. Short and made on a low budget, it is Fellini's political comment upon Italy. It shows the instrumentalists all as great individuals who cannot be disciplined by the conductor. The orchestra represents the Italian people and the unsuccessful conductor shows the inability of any government to rule the country well.

Questions

1 What are the main childhood influences which appear in Fellini's films?
2 What aspects of Italian life has Fellini satirized in his films?
3 Which of the films do you think would have been expensive to make and why?

Scene from Fellini's *Roma*

Revision: Section Four

I   Who was who?

1   Who went into exile when the 'Black' Guelf party came to power?
2   Who was sent to a village in Southern Italy as a political exile?
3   Whose name was taken as a political slogan?
4   Who wrote with 'mirror' handwriting?
5   Who wrote the 'Canticle of the Creatures'?
6   Who was taken prisoner when fighting against Perugia?
7   Who spent his last years under house arrest in Tuscany?
8   Who had been given up for lost when he returned to his native Venice?
9   Who had an Irish mother and an Italian father?

II   Multiple choice

1   Galileo was in trouble for supporting the ideas of Newton/Copernicus/Halley.
2   Aliano is in Basilicata/Calabria/Sicily.
3   St Francis of Assisi was the son of a banker/cloth merchant/mayor.
4   Fellini was born in San Marino/Ravenna/Rimini.
5   Galileo was professor at the University of Florence/Pisa/Padua.
6   Michelangelo was born at Caprese/Florence/Rome.
7   Marconi sent radio signals across the Atlantic from Cork/Sardinia/Cornwall.
8   Verdi's *Aida* was first performed at La Scala/Cairo/Venice.
9   Marco Polo did not travel through Egypt/India/Persia.

III   True or false?

1   Giuseppe Verdi's father was rich.
2   The film *Amarcord* is set in ancient Rome.
3   Dante was born in 1265.
4   Verdi was a friend of Cavour.
5   St Francis of Assisi became a Benedictine monk.
6   Leonardo da Vinci died in France.
7   'The Last Judgement' fresco is in St Peter's Basilica.
8   *La Dolce Vita* was produced in 1960.
9   Leonardo refused to have anything to do with war.
10   Michelangelo did a lot of work for Savonarola.

Final Examination

1   What is the Maremma?
2   When did Italy vote itself a republic?
3   What is *cultura promiscua*?
4   Where is the Valtellina?
5   Who was Italy's prime minister for eight years after World War 2?
6   Where is Italy's *Grand Prix* circuit?
7   Who was Mussolini's favourite mistress?
8   What language is spoken in Alto Adige?
9   When did the popes go into exile in Avignon?
10 What is the '*Osservatore Romano*'?
11 Which is Italy's second largest city?
12 What are *paglia e fieno*?
13 What is the largest fish caught in the Mediterranean?
14 Who was Charlemagne?
15 What is a *passeggiata*?
16 In which *regione* is Bologna?
17 What three books make up Dante's *La Divina Commedia*?
18 Where is Italy's largest plain?
19 Who are the *Brigate Rosse*?
20 Which is Italy's smallest *regione*?
21 What is *Il Messaggero*?
22 Where did Roger II make his capital?
23 Where is there an airport called 'Cristoforo Colombo'?
24 Where are FIAT based?
25 What was *I Vitelloni*?
26 What dominates the Plain of Catania?
27 How many channels are there on RAI television?
28 What is a *vendetta*?
29 Where are the Egadi islands?
30 Who went to Xanadu in the 13th century?
31 What happened in 1922?
32 Where did Garibaldi land when he invaded Sicily?
33 What is pasta made from?
34 What is *Est! Est!! Est!!!*?
35 How did Fascism get its name?
36 Which Roman Emperor was responsible for St Peter's death?
37 Where is Syracuse?
38 Who was Julius Caesar's adopted son and heir?
39 What are the names of Italy's *four* active volcanoes?
40 What was the significance of the village of Aliano?
41 Where is the *Palio* festival held?
42 What takes place in a *conclave*?
43 Who wrote *Tosca*?
44 Who are the 'Poor Clares'?
45 Where are there two independent states within Italy?
46 What did Dante die of?
47 Who was Francesco Crispi?
48 What are *bocce*?
49 Who wrote *il Milione*?
50 Who was pope at the time of the *Risorgimento*?

Acknowledgements

The author and publisher would like to thank the following for permission to reproduce their photographs or illustrations.

Richard Gibbs: pp. 8, 13 (bottom), 46
FIAT: p. 13 (top).
Chris Warde Jones: pp. 17 (bottom), 21 (both), 37 (top), 47 (bottom), 58 65 (bottom), 105 (bottom)
David Palmer: p. 23 (top), 41 (both)
La Repubblica: p. 61.
Barrie Spicer: pp. 25, 39 (bottom), 60 (top), 62 (top), 70
Jonathan Barrow: p. 35 (bottom right)
Geraldine Braithwaite: pp. 45, 85 (bottom), 89, 93 (bottom), 97 (top)
Mark Thompson: p. 50 (bottom)
Mark Horn: 60 (bottom)
Popperfoto: p. 66, 100, 102 (both), 103, 104
BBC Hulton Picture Library: p. 69 (both), 120, 121, 122
Cinema Bookshop: p. 71, 125
Mansell Collection: p. 83, 85 (top), 90 (bottom), 91, 92, 93 (top), 94, 95, 96, 98 (bottom), 99, 109, 110, 112, 113, 114 (both), 115, 116, 117 (both), 118 (top), 119
Michael Hill: pp. 9, 10, 11, 12, 15 (both), 16, 17 (top), 18, 19 (both) 20, 23 (bottom), 24, 26 (both), 28 (both), 30, 31 (both), 29, 32, 33 (both), 34, 35 (top and bottom left), 36, 37 (bottom), 38, 39 (top), 43, 44, 47 (top), 48, 49 (both), 50 (top), 51 (top), 52, 53, 54, 55 (both), 56, 57 (both), 59, 62 (bottom), 63, 64 (both), 65 (top), 67 (both), 68, 72 (both), 73, 75 (all), 77 (both), 78, 79, 81 (both), 82 (both), 84, 86, 87 (both), 88 (both), 90 (top), 97 (bottom), 98 (top), 101 (both), 105 (top), 118 (bottom), 123

The author and publisher would also like to thank Kate Menhinick for the recipe on p. 48 and the preparation of the typescript.

List of maps and diagrams